D1015582

Pastoral MEDIATION:
Second Edition

An Innovative Practice
Mary Kendall Hope, Ph.D.

Pax Pugna Publishing
Raleigh, North Carolina

Pax Pugna Publishing
An imprint of LuLu Press
3101 Hillsborough Street
Raleigh, North Carolina 27607

ISBN: 978-1-312-06012-8

Printed in the United States of America

Book Design: Mary Kendall Hope

Dedication

I would like to dedicate this book to
Kate & Emily my Daughters
And to My Friends, & Students of Mediation,
Conflict Resolution & Psychology.

Acknowledgements

I Would Further Like to Acknowledge the Many
Talented and Caring Mediators that I have
Worked With and Been Mentored by. Thank You For
Providing Me With the Opportunities to Mediate
And Learn Better Skills of Mediation.

For the Faculty & Staff
Of the Graduate Theological Foundation
I Would Like to Express My Appreciation
For Their Support
And Caring of My Work as a Professor and Writer.

Contents

List of Tables

Preface

Where is the God of justice?

-- Malachi 2:17

Some Thoughts on God and Justice

Faith is the substance of things hoped for, the belief in things not seen, (Hebrews 11:1). This ancient Biblical text encapsulates the stimulus for this work. I present this theory of pastoral mediation in faith that readers will accept these concepts with an open mind and an open heart. It evolved from that place inside my heart that I believe God lives, and I am often unaware of, because He moves around.

I believe God is in many places of contrast in our world and within our beings. He is in places that we would not suspect in times of conflict. He is there when unjustified tragedies occur. He is there when someone dies a painful death, or worse lives to feel the pain when it lingers.

When the negative side of conflict hits us, we may wonder; where was God – the God I wanted to be there to save me? Why did this happen? Of course, we often forget to acknowledge the good fortune that comes our way, but God is there as well.

God has been in many places of conflict for me, both personally and professionally. It is often that I have wondered where God is when a terrible crisis hits that I do not understand. I have wondered; why wasn't He bigger than this problem? Why didn't He use His power to save me and mine from such harm? I had done all that I was able to prevent the conflict, and I deserved help. I include some of my own honest thoughts here, because I suspect others feel this way at times as well, especially when conflict strikes. The ugly specter of conflict visits all of us from time to time.

Defining Justice

Where is justice in these situations? Does justice exist on a level above the conflicts that humans' experience? I am not sure. When I question what justice is and where it can be found I realize, maybe it lies within the same place that God lives. Justice, like God is everywhere, available but not always able to be held fast for the *use* we feel is deserved. There is more than one concept of justice. Even when there appears to be no "other" perspective, one exists.

Justice is a *goal* created from work between two entities in conflict. It seeks to establish a new state of being for those entities. Justice encompasses facts from both the present and the past. It seeks to reestablish order and good functioning for all who are involved in a dispute. Whenever a crisis hits, humans question the justness of the consequences. Both sides in any conflict have a perspective and for justice to be established, both perspectives must be respected equally.

Whether it is the need of an individual to rage - against a family to remain stable - or an accused criminal to go free against a system established to maintain the notion of order; justice (or the lack thereof) lies with the culmination of a hard fought battle. I believe justice can also be found in the work to *seek* understanding.

Establishing Justice in Mediation

Justice is what is sought in mediation – a just resolution for both sides equally. This is the definition of justice that guides me to write this book. The inspiration came from God, in a manner that I have an inability to describe, but fully credit to His creativity. God exists against the backdrop of all conflict and seems to live everywhere all at once, dispensing grace to both sides of conflict alike.

After every crisis, there is change, and change necessitates a new state of being that those involved were not expecting. To accept this new state of being, humans seek to establish what is most *just* from each side's perspective.

When humans find resolution with each other and a higher power, they are able to reach peace. Peace is only the first step in solidifying resolution, but when individuals find understanding and acceptance of a new state of being, they are free to recreate a stable existence from what was destroyed in conflict.

Stimulus for This Work

As a mediator who is centered in the positive power of spiritual belief and practice, I hope to offer with this work a new look into the benefits of an old habit. The habit of individuals to seek a minister in times of conflict has been a powerful ritual in our human past throughout many cultures. Mediators should not ignore this.

As I began to study this ritual (of disputants to seek spiritual guidance), it seemed to promise a fresh set of reasoning for the field of mediation. It revealed a compelling insight into the true need of humans in conflict. Disputants need to rise above their troubles and seek a higher power for both understanding and resolution. To seek the place where justice lies, and possibly, where God is for them in their time of need.

Seeking Inspiration from a Higher Power

There are many reasons for seeking spiritual inspiration in a dispute, and the motivations for doing so can teach mediators much about how to help individuals in conflict. It led me (as a mediator) back to the original ideals that formed the field of mediation.

I researched prior theory that discussed the potential concept of "pastoral mediation." My goal was to establish this new specialty in the larger field of mediation.. I found precedent, and documented my research in the chapters of this book.

My hope is that the work to establish this new specialty of mediation will serve as one-step toward guiding the larger profession of mediation back to its original ideals. In my view, the original spirit of justice that lead judges, ministers, attorneys and counselors to establish this alternative to conventional litigation is fading.

If mediators are not able to provide a practice that is different from legal document generation, then mediators are not offering much of an alternative to conventional litigation. In my experience, the practice of mediation has lost some of its original intent, and it is time to read a page from another book of inspiration.

The practice of *pastoral mediation* can be one of many options for positive resolution, and a caring pastor an instrument for stimulating an agreement that may have a better chance to promote long-term success. When the agreements made reflect a more holistic address of both material needs and emotional understanding, an environment for long term healing (*for both parties*) is established.

Overview of This Work

This new theory of pastoral mediation seeks to fit within the *specialty* framework of the larger field of Mediation. Many states offer specialties of mediation that address prevalent needs in those geographic areas.

This specialty would be more pervasive and applicable to the entire field of mediation (in all states) and potentially adaptable to all spiritual faiths. Its intent is to provide those who would seek deeper inspiration (in the resolution of their dispute) a mediator that is patient, flexible, and able to focus on mutual goals in a spirit of positive resolution.

In this work, we will first define the current practice of mediation and provide theoretical reasoning for the establishment of this new specialty of pastoral mediation. Next, a set of methods and techniques necessary for providing mediation is described in detail, for the new professional or seasoned mediator.

A new theory of mediation style, (guided) is discussed in contrast to the more popular existing styles of directive and facilitative mediation. The need of mediators to attain credentialing is explored in depth with a presentation of references for mediators (by state) to attain the most current information on mediator credentialing.

A discussion of how the concept of pastoral mediation differs from secular mediation is described with a listing of cases that may be most appropriate to both. The reasoning for the recommendations of these cases to either secular mediation or pastoral intervention is presented. A final discourse regarding what the pastoral mediation can offer to the larger practice of mediation concludes this work.

Part I

A New Specialization
In the Field of Mediation

Chapter 1

Pastoral Mediation: An Innovative Practice

The field of mediation has been a welcome alternative to the conventional practice of litigation and judicial procedure for nearly two decades in the United States. Mediation has offered individuals in conflict a method for both resolution and healing, while simultaneously providing an opportunity for written agreement.

Defining Mediation

Many members of the public have yet to accept this alternative to litigation and need to understand it. Practice a simple definition and deliver it with ease. All who *ask* may potentially request mediation or refer someone else.

Mediation is the use of a third party neutral to assist two disputing parties to reach and write an agreement that resolves their conflict. The third party neutral is the mediator. It is important that the average person understand the significance and benefit that a neutral professional brings to individuals in dispute. A neutral and caring mediator is able to guide them through a method for resolving their dispute that respects both sides equally.

Sometimes, individuals seek a friend to help them, but find that simple caring alone is not enough. A mediator is trained to handle difficulties in the resolution process and offers the skill needed to navigate through the dispute.

Poorly resolved conflicts can yield lasting negative consequences for the parities and their families.Mediation is a private professional practice. Just like other professional practices (medicine, counseling, law…), the regulation of the practice of mediation is overseen by a private entity or board that varies by state. **Disputants** are individuals who seek mediation. This term is used for the purposes of mediation training, theory, and discussion, to specify any individual or client in the mediation process.

Defining Oneself as a Professional Mediator

A **mediator** provides professional mediation to individuals who either *select* him or have been *referred* to him. To provide mediation service, one must first have completed an appropriate amount of training to mediate, and must follow an established set of techniques designed to assist disputants to resolve their conflict.

Standards for the number of hours of training needed vary from 20-40. However, the provision of mediation is best completed by an individual who has had the benefit of formalized academic training in dispute resolution.

The pastoral mediator must seek and obtain training in mediation theories, skills, and techniques. He must further practice the delivery of these skills with an experienced mediator to establish his own proficiency to mediate a dispute before he provides pastoral mediation.Degrees in dispute or conflict resolution may be obtained at the bachelor's, masters, and doctorate levels. In addition, certificates in specialized mediation training are offered at many institutions.

Court Mediation

All disputes have the distinct possibility of ending up in court at some point, no matter how well they have been mediated or how sound the agreement. Frequently, mediated agreements that stand for years have to be amended at some point.

The amendments can take place either in court or in a subsequent mediation. It is best to assume that every mediation could potentially end up in court. Exceptions to this may or may not include informal workplace mediations or international mediations of a transformative nature that address cultural and ethnic conflicts.

What Conflicts are Suitable for Mediation?

Conflicts brought to mediation have defining characteristics (that help professionals recognize the dispute as a conflict that would be best addressed through mediation). Those characteristics include

TABLE 1 Assessment Criteria for Mediation

Mediation: 7 Criteria for Assessment

1. There are <u>two</u> opposing entities. These entities are equally matched in power

2. These two entities are able to talk with one another in a reasonably respectful manner

3. Both agree to work toward the writing of an agreement in good faith

4. Both parties are informed that the mediation process will involve several meetings. Both must be available to attend all meetings

5. Both parties agree on the fees of mediation; they further agree on when and how these fees will be paid to the mediator to include the percentage of the fee that they will split.

6. Both are told that advisement by attorneys is encouraged and both agree to either *have* attorneys present (at the same time) or *not have* attorneys present. It is strongly recommended that mediation meetings will not involve the attendance of one attorney without the other (to maintain the power balance).

7. Both are aware that the inclusion of outside individuals in the mediation process is discouraged unless approved by *all* disputants. It is recommended that if one side brings another individual to mediation, the other side brings one as well to maintain the balance of power.

These seven criteria may be used to assess whether a conflict is appropriate for mediation. Other criteria for assessment exist, but these simple guidelines help the practitioner to first determine whether the dispute in question is best suited for mediation (as opposed to negotiation, counseling, arbitration, or facilitation).

Example for Criteria One

1. There are <u>two</u> opposing entities. These entities are equally matched in power.

Example – I would not place a parent-teenager dispute in mediation – but rather in counseling or pastoral counseling. The teen is unavoidably in a position of lesser power than the parent is – and thereby does not have the ability to negotiate on the same level. The same is true of any two opposing entities that are not equally matched in power due to position, gender, age, social standing, or economic status.

Disputes, which involve a power imbalance, should not be mediated because the procedures of mediation may unintentionally harm the weaker entity and worsen the conflict. Sometimes, counseling for these parties *separately* can benefit the situation. If both parities are able to represent themselves equally at a later point, joint counseling and mediation may help them resolve the dispute.

Many in both the spiritual and secular world continue to perpetuate a stigma with counseling. This is so unfortunate. Both secular and pastoral counseling can truly assist individuals in conflict.

New Specialties in Mediation

New specialties within the field of mediation are becoming commonplace. The addition of estate planning mediation, educational mediation, clerk mediation and farm nuisance mediation have been added in the state of North Carolina in the last five years. Environmental mediation has been added as a specialty in Vermont, and many other specialties exist nationwide. As the larger field of mediation has grown, the need for more diverse and specific sets of focus has been realized.

To add another specialty to this field would serve the public with an option that they are already used to. Individuals have been knocking on the door of their local pastor for help in resolving conflicts for centuries. To provide a theoretical concept for a pastor to utilize when helping individuals in conflict, only enhances this profession's ability to serve the public.

Pastoral Mediation

The concept of pastoral mediation was pioneered by a number of innovative ministers in the United States, who were credentialed as mediators and simultaneously trained as evangelical leaders. The most prominent of these in my research was Tim Emerick-Cayton (1993).

In his book, *Divorcing with dignity*, Emerick-Cayton writes specifically about his own journey as a secular mediator and describes how his practice of mediation evolved slowly over time into a practice of "pastoral mediation" (Emerick-Cayton, 1993, p. 3).

Pastoral mediation is the practice of mediation by a pastor who has been thoroughly trained in the techniques of mediation. Pastors who mediate are usually credentialed to mediate as well, by a private entity within the state in which they intend to provide mediation service.

The credentialing of a professional pastoral mediator is the same as it would be for any outside professional (non-attorney). In most states, however, the regulations guiding the credentialing of mediation professionals differ.

The practice of pastoral mediation is just beginning to blossom upon the writing of this book. Many individuals do not immediately seek legal professionals, but do seek professional ministers. The use of evangelical leadership provides an opportunity for the provision of a more positive and transformative type of mediation for individuals in conflict. Pastoral mediation focuses on mutually positive objectives and provides disputants a more balanced and holistic resolution.

Training Pastoral Mediators

It is crucial for pastoral mediators to become credentialed. The credentialing process creates an atmosphere of consistent training and accountability and gives the pastor the validity and reliability standards of measure that he will need to withstand any questions of credibility.

It further insures that those individuals obtaining mediation services from pastors get a more consistent service that they can rely on. Many "moonlighting" professionals seek to supplement their income by becoming a mediator. However, the ramifications of poor mediation practice are far reaching. Therefore, credibility for mediators and for those who would seek mediation service is crucial. The ability to provide good reliable service is imperative to new professionals in any field and even more important in a field that has yet to be fully established in the mainstream vernacular.

The basic requirements of mediation provision will be covered in successive chapters in this book. This work, (as well as a thorough mediation-training program that includes other respected theoretical and practical manuals for mediation provision) can serve as an effective resource for a new pastoral mediator.

Entities that Oversee Mediation Provision

Each state has a different entity that oversees the practice of mediation. Some states are still in the process of developing a singular entity and set of standards that guides the practice of mediation throughout the state. There is little if any consistency in either the provision of mediation practice or training of professional mediators from state to state.

The entities that oversee mediation in each state are private organizations and not state sponsored or state governed. They sometimes bear the name of the state, for instance, the Vermont Judiciary, but they are not officially state funded nor state governed.

These organizations are frequently connected to each state's court system, either through their state bar association or state supreme court. This is because state statutes often address the provision of "court" mediation (see definition below) just as they often address the provision of law.

Mediation: A Burgeoning Profession

New professionals in the field of mediation grow exponentially each year; however, the quality of professionals entering the field appears to be suffering at the expense of high quantities of new mediators. Forty-hour training programs abound, but the skills of caring and empathetic listening are difficult to train. The experience of counselors and pastoral leaders is better suited to those in conflict.

As a certified mediator of many years, I can attest to the existence of a wide disparity in mediation qualification. The preparation, ability, and professionalism among the mediators I have worked with over two states ranges from beginner to seasoned professional, but by far the largest number of mediators in the field that I have encountered are newcomers. The motivation of easy money appears to stimulate a large number of both attorney and non-attorney professionals to become mediators. However, the true talent to affect good, lasting resolutions is scarce, and the staying power of these new mediators in the field is limited.

The Skills of Good Mediation

The ability to excel in the skill of assisting disputants to write resolutions that effectively meet disputants' *needs* makes the difference. Mediators who are able to provide good skilled delivery of mediation techniques stay in the profession. Those that are not able to provide good mediation services leave the profession.

Over the years, I began to witness an unusual phenomenon. Some of the best mediators I knew were formerly or presently ministers. I realized this one day when a friend asked me to refer him to a *good* mediator. Two names came to mind. Both were former ministers.

The feedback I received from individuals that I referred to these mediators was always positive. Individuals always commented upon the specialized skill that these individuals had. They commented how the mediator in question promoted a resolution that resolved their conflict rather than leaving them with more conflict.

Former Ministers as Mediators

After several occurrences of this, I began to realize that the skills needed to become a minister and the skills needed to become a mediator were similar. When I reviewed resolutions crafted from the mediators who had been ministers, I noted that their resolutions were the most caring, holistic, lasting, and thorough. These mediators had explored a method of inspiring spirituality with people. I was taken aback by this at first. Then later as I thought more about the qualities that comprised a holistic resolution, I found this an interesting insight.

From a popular perspective, to take a dispute to a minister seemed almost a cliché. However, embedded in every cliché is strand of unmistakable truth. Talking to a minister instead of an outside professional is the most popular method most people seek first.

If the reason individuals sought ministers in times of conflict were because they felt more cared about when they talked to a minister, then possibly *frame of mind* was key to affecting the best resolution. Ministers approached the conflict in a positive frame of mind, filled with respect for both individuals. This frame of mind was role-modeled to the disputants and transformed the resolution from the beginning. By maintaining that positive focus on goals and respect, the atmosphere of the discussions changed from combativeness to cooperation.

Adding the Specialty of Pastoral Mediation

The addition of this new specialization only enhances this profession's potential to better address conflicts. The larger field of professional mediation needs continued adaptation and improvement if it is to continue to exist as an effective and timely alternative to litigation. To listen to the call from the public for *ministers* in times of conflict connects the supply to the demand. Any business or profession that ignores changes in demand fails. In recent years, mediation has failed to gain the recognition it needs to address conflicts. It has further failed to live up to the aspirations of its original theorists. It is time to explore new inspiration for improvement.

Chapter 2

Pastoral Divorce Mediation

Families in conflict have sought mediation either by choice or by referral since the early to mid 1970's. Select regions of the United States began to develop the practice of mediation in the decade before, but it took years for the profession to gain acceptance and a consistent mode of practice. Slowly, the beginning of a new profession was forged in states throughout the nation and referrals of divorce cases to mediation began.

Divorce Mediation

Divorce Mediation addresses the specific dispute between two opposing spouses for divorce or potential divorce. Divorce mediation encompasses the division of property as well as the custody and visitation of children born of the marriage in question. Sub-categories of divorce mediation can be labeled as either "family financial" mediation or "child custody" mediation, according to the state the divorce takes place in.

Historically, the option of *mediating* the intricacies of a divorce case offered individuals in such disputes more time and consideration of complicated issues. Judges immediately recognized the benefit of such an option to disputing family members, as the court system seldom allowed for the address of intricate detail.

The need to provide families a safe place to work through family problems slowly gained acceptance from the public. Several states established mediation centers, where individuals could seek alternative dispute resolution services. Some of the first locations of mediation centers were in minister's chambers in churches. The church environment evoked an atmosphere of trust and comfort that those experiencing conflict instinctively sought.

Divorces often brought out tremendous pain and challenge, and when left unresolved, the consequences were felt by all involved. Children in these divorce cases seemed to fare the worst, their emotions and needs had no forum for consideration.

Over time, the need to remedy this sad state of dispute resolution became apparent, and local *community* mediation centers received their first sets of referrals from individuals seeking divorce mediation.

Divisions of Divorce Mediation

As more and more individuals found their way into the divorce mediation process, the areas that needed improvement and expansion became apparent. Divorce mediation dealt with two diametrically opposed objectives. The distribution of properties held by a married couple and the custody and visitation of children required two different methods of resolution because they addressed two completely different sets of problems.

In the state of North Carolina, it soon became apparent that property distribution and child custody was too much for a singular mediation. Thereby, in North Carolina (as well as in several other states) divorce mediation was divided into two categories: family financial mediation and child custody mediation.

Custody issues were often filled with emotions and complicated problems of visitation. Property division focused disputants on fair and equitable distribution of material possessions. Both types of divorce issues were of paramount importance to disputants, and both needed primary focus, yet the need to give validation to the emotional attributes of child custody while simultaneously focusing on property disputes became too much for a singular mediation. When disputants attempted to address both sets of issues at the same time, one set of issues did not get resolved as well.

A third problem arose later, when divorcing parents needed help to under stand how their decisions would affect their children. The need to educate both parents on how to parent children after a divorce was realized when a sad pattern began to emerge in the court system. Many children of divorce ended up arrested or in need of counseling.

Child custody mediation was separated into is own subcategory of divorce mediation in North Carolina, California and many other states, child custody mediation deals with the education of newly divorced parents and legal custody and visitation issues. In the states of California and North Carolina, child custody mediation has become the first component of the child custody divorce process.

Separate mediators are trained and hired in the North Carolina district court system to provide education to parents about how to parent their child(ren) following the divorce. In addition, child custody mediation continues after this education of the parents (in the state of North Carolina) to assist parents in all of the matters pertaining to the legal residence, custody, and visitation of children.

Property settlement mediation or "family financial" mediation in North Carolina was separated out from child custody mediation to allow disputants to focus on the issues surrounding the division of all properties common to the divorcing couple. Properties in question include the home, all joint possessions, debts, automobiles, bank accounts, insurance policies, retirement accounts and investments common to both disputants. Family financial or property distribution mediation assists disputants to allocate the ownership of all of these properties to include future disbursements and debt payments to both parties in a manner that is fair, equitable, and acceptable to both.

Differences between the States: Divorce Mediation

The Association for Conflict Resolution began an endeavor to unify the training and provision of mediation in 2001. However, upon the writing of this book, the work to complete this process has not been realized. It is likely that the ACR will systematically establish consistent protocols for both mediator credentialing and provision, but this process will take a considerable amount of time.

The differences in the provision of divorce mediation vary as widely as there are states in the U.S. Each state's domestic or family court system processes cases of divorce mediation but does not regulate its practice. In some states, the provision of divorce mediation differs by county and region as well. Another difference between state provisions of mediation occurs in the training of mediators.

Some states "certify" mediators, while others use much of the same training criteria to "register" mediators. This subject will be explored in detail in chapter eleven of this book. The need for professional mediators to undergo a credentialing process prior to providing divorce mediation remains constant.

Improving Divorce Mediation

Divorce mediation was theorized on the premise that with work and time, better methods for restoring peace to families existed. The pursuit of better forms of mediation that more efficiently address *both* the emotional and financial needs of divorcing families continues.

At the onset of the provision of divorce mediation, pastors were among the first professional mediators. People trusted pastors to intervene in crisis. Their experience of being there for families in times of trouble lent credibility to professional ministers, victors, bishops, rectors, and other evangelical leaders.

Mediation at the Turn of the 21st Century

At the turn of the 21st century, the provision of divorce mediation continues to differ by state. Many states separate divorce mediation by property division and child custody, but some states continue to tackle both sets of issues simultaneously. Either method has the potential of addressing the issues of divorce mediation well, but the need to provide validation and a separate focus for the emotional components of child custody and visitation is a clear benefit to disputants and their families.

As the demand for divorce mediation continues to increase from court referrals and the public. Disputants need mediators that are able to focus on the emotional aspects of their dispute. Pastoral divorce mediators would be better equipped to focus disputants on *positive mutual goals* that promote a more holistic resolution. Their background of evangelical training and focus on spiritual reconciliation uniquely qualify them to assist divorcing couples to approach their conflict with a more collaborative mindset. The challenge is to train pastors appropriately to provide this highly skilled service.

Chapter 3

That you will do us no harm, just as we did not harm you, but always treated you well and sent you away in peace.

- Genesis 29:26

Pastoral Mediation: First Do No Harm

Unbeknownst to most of us, the Hippocratic Oath (that historically guided the induction of new medical doctors into practice) does not contain this phrase. "First, do no harm," is a paraphrase of the statements contained in this ancient set of oaths, inspired by Socrates.

The meaning of this directive continues to strike a deep truth in all of us who read it. Our medical physicians hold an oft times "life and death" power over our lives to both help and harm us. We all hope that their frame of reference is to seek first to heal us, rather than taking risks that may harm us.

"First do no harm" is the public's hope for both medical and psychological providers. It should be the first rule for mediators as well. All of these professionals (doctors, attorneys, counselors…) have the potential to harm us. Mediators may harm by enabling an abuser or more powerful person *or group* to gain more recognition. Both sides in a dispute interpret recognition as validation.

Defining Harm

To "harm" implies an intentional act to hurt another. Sometimes, harm is misperceived by an individual, but this does not mean that the hurt is any less detrimental. To *begin* to heal from a perceived emotional harm, the individual must first become aware that the intention to harm was not present. If the intention to harm is present, then a process of forgiveness is necessary for healing. Remember, forgiveness can often take time and may slow the individual's ability to objectively work through a problem. Sometimes, it is best to take a break and come back to the mediation after a perception of harm is realized (from either the other disputants or the mediator).

As mediators, both secular and pastoral, we must always seek first to do no harm. Whether intentional or unintentional, a perception of hurt deepens a conflict. A professional pastor, intent on providing help by *definition* does not seek to harm. How then could a pastoral mediator harm? A pastoral mediator would intend to provide the best of care and spirituality. The pastoral mediator by definition should be above the secular mediator in not inflicting harm.

However, here is where I (as a professional mediator) become the most concerned. The pastoral mediator, by his very distinction as such, has the ability to *unintentionally* harm in a far deeper capacity than the secular mediator.

A man or woman of God, with the best intentions may actually pose a greater risk of harm to disputants. When one is approached by the devil in red, the sting of his fire is expected. When one is approached by a messenger in white, a sting coming invisibly cuts deeper, especially if the messenger is bearing a "sting" and is *unaware* of it.

A pastoral mediator would inevitably provide service to the best of his ability. However, if the pastoral mediator's ability is limited in mediation skill and technique, he may tear open a deeper infection, instead of applying the proper care and ointment to the wound already present.

The pastoral mediator truly comes into the profession of mediation at a slight disadvantage. His forte comes from the innate skills that may not be able to be "taught" to another professional. However, in leaning on these abilities too heavily and not taking the proper time and care to attain good mediation skill and credentials, the pastoral mediator may indeed harm the disputants that he seeks so earnestly to help.

"Interveners" into a conflict (those seeking to help) can *always* make the situation worse and cause far greater harm than good, while all the time implementing the skills required. For it is not just the "skills" themselves, but *how* they are applied.

Damage by Omission

Pastoral mediators may misinterpret information or omit mediation steps and thereby cause damage by omission. If a pastoral mediator focuses too keenly on his own spiritual interpretation of events while disputants expend precious energy telling him information, he may miss valuable opportunities to gain objective insight into the deeper issues presented. Disputants are not likely to repeat painful information twice, because it hurts to say it even once. Disputants also avoid pain by changing the subject or may defer their own ability to tackle their issues by asking *you* what to do.

Disputants seek to avoid pain, and it is natural for a minister to wish to alleviate pain, and skip a guiding principle of mediation. Mediators do not give advice or solve problems. It is best to empower disputants to the ability that God gives us to handle pain and deal with the problems presented rather than omit this opportunity to encourage them to seek options. By empowering disputants to solve their problems, you "teach them to fish," rather than give them the answers.

Secular mediators make "damage by omission" errors as well. Often, secular mediators fail to acknowledge the good that may be gained from considering a more holistic resolution (from the disputants' perspective). It is good to learn the value of both lessons. Mediate slowly with God's patience and God's love.

Second, Provide Skill that Truly Helps

This brings to mind the second implication for this chapter. First, do no harm; second, provide skill that truly helps the disputants (Croft, 1964). The nice day for the mediator is when he goes home feeling warm and cozy inside. If you go home feeling warm and cozy inside *every* day as a mediator, I would hazard to state; you are not truly helping those you are serving. You are making them "feel nice," about you, maybe even about their situations. That is a benefit to *you*.

To benefit those you serve, you must have the courage to bring up the difficult subjects and have the patience to allow the disputants to tell their story and resolve their own emotions. Trust yourself as a practitioner; trust the disputants to be able to handle the pain they feel. If you truly want to help those who come to see you for help, listen and care; this will go a long way toward stimulating them to heal.

Strong Enough to Handle the Ugly

If you stick to warm fuzzy conversations, people will *tell* you that they really like you. What they will wish is - that they had really *dealt* with the hardest part of their problem that day in mediation. They will wish that they had had the courage to deal with the part that was too ugly to talk about, to hard to say, too embarrassing or difficult to find words to describe.

They will pray that you could help them envision a time that others could understand the *worst part* and forgive them for it, so they can forgive themselves.They will respect you deeply if you have the courage to help them face the ugly side of their fears and their problems with the love of God. They need someone to stimulate a renewed inner strength in them, so that they can help themselves handle the changes that life has brought them.

Do *know* that all persons (practitioners and disputants) who work valiantly to deal with conflicts need days that they feel *good* (when they go home) as well. These days give the disputants the energy and encouragement to do the continued work. Just like any form of positive reinforcement though, feeling good about the work done in mediation is much more treasured when the *hard* work (of resolving the conflict) happens simultaneously. It creates an environment of appreciation of the pleasant experiences gained through small successes in mediation.

If you wish to become a pastoral mediator, secular mediator, or any kind of counselor or helping person, know first what people truly need of you. They need you to be strong enough to handle the ugly part of life – to talk about these ugly issues as if they are *not* taboo – and to inspire them to recover from the problems that they used to think that they could not handle. It is a selfless and thankless job while you are going through it. Later, those you help will thank you many times in silence.

Thankless Job

If you have selected this specialty of pastoral mediation in hopes of the true recognition that you feel you have always deserved but never had the privilege of, I am here to tell you that you have selected the wrong profession. If you want and need recognition, then you likely *do* need it and deserve it. Become a national evangelist, and you will be able to minister to the masses and receive the recognition you deserve.

If you choose to become a pastoral mediator and are fortunate enough to be blessed by God with the ability to do it well, people will rarely recognize how much your hard work has helped them. They will not notice that you asked the question or that it was the right question. They will not notice who stimulated the healing that helped them begin a process of real resolution.

They will think that they did it themselves, and rarely (if ever) give you credit for the worry and sweat that you did (on the other side of the room) thinking up that *one sentence* you could get in edgewise. I know this because I have been that person, on both sides.

To help another person in need, without the promise of thanks or recognition is a gesture of pure love, the kind of love God meant for us all to display for one another, but so often don't.

To truly learn and practice the skills of mediation with an unbiased consistency of God's grace takes tremendous dedication and strength. Most days are exhausting and professionals must have sharp skills and remain clearly focused in the positive goals of mediation.

Mediation Free from Bias

The pastoral counselor and pastoral mediator must be free from conscious bias. We all strive to be aware of our own personal biases, values, etc... as professional counselors and mediators - especially - as pastoral counselors and/or pastoral mediators.
To every extent possible, we must not let our personal biases ever affect our professional service. When one does become aware of a bias that may innocently exist – one must be completely honest with oneself and graciously refer the disputant(s) to another provider.

This should not be an embarrassing occurrence. It is commonplace for professionals to recommend other specific providers. A specially trained practitioner may be just what the disputants need. Consider how often medical doctors refer patients to a specialist. Referral is the way to handle a situation involving a "bias" or pre-existing relationship. To continue to see a disputant whom one had discovered biases with – would hurt the process of resolution for everyone involved, because the resolution would be influenced by the bias.

Spiritual Values & Beliefs

Pastoral counselors *often* find themselves dealing with the issues surrounding personal spiritual values and beliefs. The same can be true for pastoral mediators. In comparison to secular mediators, pastoral mediators are likely to know those they counsel, and because the disputants may be members of their congregation. Pastoral discussions inevitably are grounded in spiritual values and beliefs that may differ *or* may be the same as the disputants.

Values and beliefs are personal, as our relationship with God is personal. However, as a pastoral counselor or pastoral mediator, the professional must envision a "line" in each instance in which a personal value and belief may come into conflict with a value of a disputant. He must "see" and/or find that line of caring objectivity and remain on the safe side of it.

For example, if one of the disputants' has engaged in an outside marital affair that is revealed for the first time during the mediation, the mediator may have personal beliefs or values that may cause him to have negative feelings toward one disputant. Another mediator may choose to draw a professional "line" of objectivity and not consider the past mistakes of the disputant, but rather focus on how to assist these individuals to resolve their present circumstances. In essence, the mediator removes his own judgment, saving this for God's wisdom.

Taking a Break & Referrals

To remove personal spiritual values, is one of the most selfless and caring things a pastoral counselor or pastoral mediator will do for the disputant. When a mediator's personal values and beliefs do come into conflict with disputants' stated values and beliefs, it is best for the mediator to be honest about this with himself in silence and either end the mediation or (at the very least) take a break that day.

A break will give the mediator time to consider whether he can continue to provide objective mediation service. If the mediator finds that he can no longer provide mediation that is free from his own objections to the disputants' *opposing* values and beliefs, then the mediator should refer the disputants to another mediator.

It is best to *not* disclose the reasons for referral. Personal values, beliefs, and interpretations of spiritual concepts can vary greatly and cause unneeded offense. As in a congregational situation, it is still possible to maintain a good relationship with individuals that you disagree with. As Christian teachings remind us, "judge not, lest ye be judged" (Matthew 7: 1). "Though the wicked exalt themselves against them, the Lord will be the final judge of all men. He will promote and He will cast down. We must look to Him and not to man," (Psalms 75:10).

Your experience of religion and spirituality will be different from every other person on earth in some capacity or another. We all deserve the respect God granted to us of having a personal spiritual relationship with Him, and we are instructed that "Do not judge, so that you may not be judged, for with the judgment you make; you will be judged, and the measure you give will be the measure you get," (Matthew 7: 1-3).

In the Eye of the Beholder

Harm is in the "eye of the beholder," (Hamilton, 2008; 1878). In mediation, to respect the perspective of the disputants is paramount. To ascertain and understand why disputants feel harm (either from the other party or potentially from the mediator) is key to keeping a mediation proceeding healthfully.

The disputant in conflict comes into the process in a level of moderate to severe pain already. When another hurt is placed on top of this, the additional perceived hurt (and perception IS reality – in terms of pain) builds on what is already present. Harm inflicted unintentionally by a mediator can be worse than the initial pain experienced by the conflict or at very least, it can be just as great.

If one experiences *another* laceration to the arm by accident from a rescue worker – the pain is double for the victim, regardless of how it happened. The thing to do is clear. Go back, as efficiently as possible and repair the damage. Clean the "wound" by stating your error and apologizing for any confusion or lapse in communication. Continue the mediation. Wounds can heal quickly if treated well at the *first* indication of hurt.

Mediation Can Make a Conflict Worse

Mediators often make conflicts worse. Sometimes, making a problem worse is unavoidable because the wound is so infested with past build up of pain and trauma that things have to get worse before they can get better. For example, if one opens a wound, festering with infection, the wound is likely to hurt severely when opened. The release of the infection is ugly, unpleasant, and sometimes painful. Festered wounds that have been opened sometimes get worse. It is a risk a person has to take to relieve the danger the infection poses to the rest of the body. Infections have the potential of poisoning the bloodstream of the entire being. The same is true of mediation. A mediator opens a conflict "wound" and exposes all the pain within to the "treatment" the mediator and disputants apply to help heal the conflict wounds.

Opening the Conflict Wound

Sometimes, wounds that have festered for years and years without attention run the risk of getting into the "bloodstream" of the entire family. Digging into any wound always carries just as much potential of worsening the infection as relieving it. To open a conflict, and truly help that conflict, the professional must open it deep enough to let the pain of the infection out and apply positive words to promote healing.

Often, serious conflict wounds have already begun to "infect" the family system (of children, grandparents, siblings, and friends) that surrounds it. Any conflict that has affected a family has influenced all of its family members. The severity of the affect is the question. The most severe conflicts have progressed beyond the simple arguments that the disputants will originally present to you.

Make no mistake; a child (who is peripherally involved in an adult conflict) who has argued repeatedly with his parents is experiencing a serious side affect of the conflict. These surface level arguments present telltale signs of deeper conflict. As a mediator, accept what you hear. Remember that disputants often tell you exactly what the problem is on the first meeting. They begin with the surface of the conflict wound. Listen for the deeper aspects, but avoid placing your own interpretations on their problems. Unfortunately, things can be much worse than disputants *present*. Usually, when adults finally seek mediation, the problem is its most severe to date.

Allow them the time they need to discover their own truths, revelations, options and ultimately solutions. Never impose your own, even if they ask you. Disputants are able to find their own solutions. Believe this. As God trusts you to find your own truths, so trust them. Separate yourself as minister from mediator. Save your sermons for the pulpit. Use God's patience and love that he has granted to you to listen, care, and ask gentle questions.

Guiding Mandate for All Pastoral Mediators

Because pastors carry a dual role of "minister" and "mediator", they face a role distinction challenge from the inception of the mediation process. My advisement to you is to *clearly* distinguish for yourself your own boundaries of professional service when you provide pastoral mediation.

Just as you would distinguish your interactions in church with your congregate from your interactions with them in a public grocery store, consider how you will conduct yourself differently in mediation. Know where your role as a minister ends and where your role as a mediator begins. Start with listening. Work by listening and caring. Finish by listening.

Mediation is a powerful mechanism for the transfer of God's love and grace – which is big enough to cover us all. God's grace will be there for you as a mediator, as you learn this craft and seek first to help and not harm.

Part II

Methods of Mediation
Practice

Chapter 4

For it is God who works in you to will and to act according to His good purpose.

- Philippians 2:13

The Power of Positive Focus

When disputants enter into mediation, they come to you (their mediator) from a place of negativity. No matter how courteous and respectful they may be, inside, they have feelings of conflict, confusion, pain, disappointment, anger, guilt, and often jealousy and vengeance.

We all have these emotions at our easy disposal, and if we are honest with ourselves, we all have "sinned and fallen short of the glory." Conflict brings out the worst of our negative thoughts, feelings, and emotions.

The Negative Challenge of Conflict

Conflicts strike deep at the heart of what is most precious to us, and conflicts challenge us within an inch of our tolerance. These challenges to our tolerance define the problems that face us as a "conflict."

Problems, by their very definition have no solutions readily apparent, and require new, untested paradigms to be forged from the deep "forests" of tradition, habit, comfort and familiarity that exist in our lives. Our very pathways of survival have to be re-written to overcome most conflicts. These prospects are daunting, and are the same prospects that face those coming to us for help.

The "Can't Do *That*" Syndrome

Disputants have a very great fear of traversing these overgrown "jungles" of tradition in their lives. They tell themselves that they "can't change this" or "won't do it," and subsequently, they cannot do it.

Until an individual gets to a place in his own frame of mind that allows him to empower himself, he actually cannot change. He has imprisoned his own self in handcuffs in his mind – preventing himself from even considering what a "change" could look like – and dooming his next set of interactions to the I "can't do *that*" syndrome.

Individuals in conflict prevent themselves from utilizing the power they have to embrace the options that exist to their problems. They are both *aware* of some options and *unaware* of many other available alternatives that could be pursued. They see unfamiliar alternatives as untested, frightening, difficult, and unappealing. You may hear them deem these suggestions as "not an option," initially, but silently, they may be considering what they have heard.

They subsequently repeat to themselves, at every opportunity for consideration, "I can't do that." Having stated this to themselves as true, they continue to believe this faulty thinking that brought them to you in the first place. Pride is an ugly obstacle that a mediator can easily recognize, but a disputant finds invisible. Pride tends to be the most common cause and persistent obstacle of the "I can't do that," syndrome. Take heart, disputants remember the suggestions made.

Give them time to consider what was suggested. Allow them to bring it up again. Listen. Allow them to change their mind without "losing face." (See saving face below) When you allow disputants the respect of declaring that they "can't do that", you give them the freedom to consider how this *could* be possible. They may or may *not* change their mind later, but they are likely to consider other options if they stay engaged in the mediation.

Methods of Positive Focus

As a mediator of many years, I have found that confronting this "pride" head on – naming it as such and requesting a different consideration - frequently does NOT work as a sole confrontation method. Often, it is best to agree with the disputant and go along his path of reasoning until its end.

Then, the disputant is free to uncover new options and realize a new perception of these options on his own which is much more powerful and salient to him. It is a repeated occurrence for me that this exercise reveals to the disputant a way of selecting an option that *before* mediation, he would not have considered.

These discoveries work best when the *disputan*t does the discovering and the options are not simply *provided* by the mediator. The mediator's job is to leave breadcrumbs, by asking open-ended questions and allow the disputants to uncover their own path. You do not need to lead disputants too much, because they are already there. In fact, they are deeply embedded and invested in the specifics of the conflict - much more than you are.

Maintaining Boundaries & Saving Face

When disputants enter the resolution process, their self-image is made up of their self-composure, sense of boundaries, self-esteem, identity and self-confidence. Without a measure of strength, the individual is defenseless and will be too vulnerable to affect an equitable resolution. It is important for the mediator to understand that each individual needs their personal identity to remain in tact while discussing issues of conflict, especially during the beginning of the mediation process.

In fact, to maintain a good identity throughout the mediation process is crucial for both disputing sides. This will insure an equitable resolution that has a better chance of generalizing to all aspects of their lives, and becoming a resolution that is sustainable over time. As the mediation gets into a work phase, elements of each disputant's personal identity will be challenged as he works to "save face." It is important to help disputants 'save face,' or maintain their self-respect, personal boundaries, self-esteem, and self-confidence as they work to re-define what is and is *not* acceptable in a mediated agreement. A good mediated agreement will challenge every aspect of a disputant's personal identity. When the mediator assists the disputant to maintain his personal identity (while accepting the changes inherent in the mediation process), the possibilities for successful compromise begin to build on one another to affect a resolution.

The Power of a Positive Perspective

To assist disputants to accomplish a more sustainable and holistic agreement, the mediator must always stay focused in a positive perspective. As disputants challenge former definitions of themselves they will constantly be tempted to doubt their own ability to grow.

Disputants will first deny their negative feelings, while simultaneously *shooting down* the possibility of changing well-established habits, traditions, methods, and rules that they have used for years.

Whether these habits have yielded successful results or not, they are "tradition" to the disputant and letting go of tradition is always a significant challenge. To delve into the unknown and (for them) untested is an activity that provokes unspoken fear, and often provokes the "I can't do that" syndrome. By keeping a positive focus (in your responses, reactions and all active listening skills) you will be able to consistently assist the disputant to challenge his own beliefs (that are not working for him). What disputants are not aware of is, the answer to their problems lies in changing the very behavioral patterns that they want most to hold on to and know least about how to change.

How to Deal with Negative Feelings

Disputants usually come into the mediation with very negative thoughts and feelings about the opposing party. They have a great deal of pent up anger, resentment and disappointment, and they often seek first to blame the other side for their conflict. Both parties in a dispute have the same feelings, though some express these negative feelings with anger, while others express themselves through sadness and sometimes do not express these feelings out loud at all. Both have much guilt to overcome and neither is open to letting go of their perspective. To begin mediation with this set of variables presents a problem to the mediator from the word go. Often, new mediators begin the step-by-step process of mediation, expecting each stage to work as originally intended. However, these behaviors come in no particular order and with random appearance and re-appearance:

- the sting of animosity,
- denial,
- non-compliance,
- lack of cooperation,
- confusion,
- rejection of assistance,
- non-attendance (to mediation),
- and a general state of silence that often conveys misplaced anger and blame.

All of these extremely negative thoughts, feelings, intentions, behaviors and generally pervasive emotions may be present at any point in the mediation. Some negative emotions will be present in varying forms and will show up in various strengths and for intermittent durations. In addition, a number of the negative emotions listed above will show up *simultaneously* and have no clear cause or connection to the problems being discussed.

As a mediator, you should expect all of these factors. Sometimes, negative emotions will be severe and will persist. If this happens, take heart, you are doing a good job so far. You have been successful in opening a wound that needs to let infection out. Your job is to stand fast. Do not react just listen.

Role-model strength and empathy in your very limited responses. You may need to share a very brief story – hypothetical but related. Then ask a single open-ended question and provide a safe place for them to respectfully let out what they are feeling. Give each side the same time to speak. If you stay strong and positive, this will change the negativity *and* entire status of the conflict.

Keeping a Positive Focus through the Worst of the Conflict

Disputes (as mentioned in the previous chapter) are like infected wounds. Some run deep; others run very deep. For our purposes, all wounds that end up in mediation also have infection. When one is treating an infection, to open or not open the wound is a question needing professional guidance. Most doctors recommend that if the "white" of the infection is at the top – easy to be touched and seen, then it is best to open the wound and allow the bacteria to drain.

The next stage is crucial, but applies to not only wounds but conflicts as well. Be patient. Do not push. Allow plenty of time for the negative emotions to emerge in an atmosphere of caring, safety, and acceptance.

Allow the "bacteria" (or negative emotions) to release gently and cleanly. This alone, when repeated and patiently attended to, will begin the healing process. The "medicine" of caring response and caring acceptance (as outlined more specifically in chapter six) will stimulate the body to begin a restorative process, replacing old, infected cells with newer, healthier "versions" of the body's own cells. The same is true for the former faulty behaviors and negative emotions that are released in a good mediation.

Taking a New "Picture"

Our physical bodies go through this process daily, as cells "take pictures" of themselves and replicate. The "picture" they take (to replicate a new day's cells) depends on what we have done to affect these cells during that day. What we eat, drink, rub on, scrub on, or medicate with *all* impacts these daily "pictures" our cells take to make our body "new" again for another day. When individuals in a dispute come into the mediation process, their conflict has the same set of opportunities for renewal and re-growth.

What we (the disputants and mediator together) "do" to the wounds brought (and sometimes opened) has the opportunity each day of "changing the picture," of the conflict. As negative emotions come out and come into contact with caring responses and support, they have the opportunity to heal, just a little, every day.

Mediators focused in a positive set of responses and caring acceptance can promote this slow, steady healing. Resolutions that are based in kindness and mutual respect are more likely to be maintained and have a greater opportunity for sustainability.

Saving Face, Saving Grace

Stimulating disputants to be kind and caring is a challenge. Often, these individuals may need time to work through issues separately in counseling before they are able to create an agreement based in mutual respect. The negative emotions that exist in mediation must be allowed to come forth in a supportive atmosphere. If negative emotions begin to dominate the mediation, then it is best to take a break.

The most severe and persistent flows of negative emotion (beyond two or more days of mediation) may need a referral to counseling. Referring a disputant to counseling must be done in complete privacy. It can be done in a spirit of caring and support rather than allowing these times and moments to weaken one side's personal identity – and thereby status in the mediation.
Saving face is one of the most important aspects of preserving the power balance in mediation. Assuring that the discussion is "equitable" is one of your most important tasks as a mediator. To refer without bias, but with genuine caring is beneficial to both sides. Referrals handled properly preserve the respect of the mediation process. Refer with discretion and always outside of the other's knowledge. Schedule

the next session of mediation at time that allows for counseling to occur. To assign an outside task in addition to the counseling would serve to "save face" for disputants needing resolve deep negative feelings. A mediator could ask both disputants to seek additional information for other aspects of the mediation, in order to "save face" for the individual(s) who may also seek counseling during this break between mediation sessions.

Most mediators are able to allow time for the resolution of negative emotions by taking breaks for lunch or caucuses (see chapters five-nine). As a mediator, assure to do everything in your power to help the disputants experiencing moments of vulnerability to "save face." When you do so, you will empower them to complete the mediation.

Loaves & Fishes

Mediation is focused solely on assisting disputants in the resolution of a very specific set of problems – at a very specific time in their life. Do not address *all* of the problems in a disputant's life. Good mediation focuses disputants on one or two well-defined problems. To resolve one problem well, can be a disputant's turning point. It allows him or her to build a foundation for the successful resolution of other problems within their dispute and indeed within their lives.

Learning to resolve problems one at a time is like the parable of the loaves and the fishes Jesus used when teaching the disciples. The crowds were hungry and the disciples asked 'how can we feed them all?' Jesus wisely fed them on fish and serving of bread at a time. With two fishes and five loaves, he fed the multitude, not because he set out to feed them all at once. He simply began one meal at a time, and the supply to feed the rest, manifested itself from God (Matthew 14: 13-21).

Chapter 5

Dear children, let us not love with words or tongue but with actions and in truth.

- 1 John 3:18

Listening From a Caring Perspective

Pastors have a great capacity to provide a deep sense of caring. This caring goes a long way toward effective listening, empathy, and ultimately toward successful resolution and healing

Listening: The Most Important Objective

Disputants first need to be listened to and second, need to be listened to. The repeat of this priority reveals the depth of need. When disputants feel that they have been understood, they *begin* the slow process of healing. Given that listening is the most important skill of mediation, it is necessary to become familiar with the other skill objectives for the mediating professional.

TABLE 2   Three Skilled Tasks

A Mediator Serves the Disputants Through
Three Skilled Tasks that he or she is solely responsible for:
1. Listening well
2. Responding skillfully, and
3. Patiently writing the agreement

This chapter contains a variety of techniques, and it is important to understand that a mediator does not need to micromanage the mediation by implementing each perfectly. The skilled mediator simply knows the technique he uses, but simultaneously remains focused on the key elements of mediation. The three skills from Table five encompass the repeated tasks of mediation, so as we explore the more detailed techniques, keep in mind that a mediator returns to these three tasks as he conducts the mediation.

When the mediator becomes skilled, he will find that in the larger scheme of things, he needs to focus on these three skilled tasks and **repeat** them as often as the disputants need these. This focus will help those in conflict to both reach and write an agreement of resolution. Many times, the mediator will need to go from writing the agreement to listening and responding again.

He will then need to re-write the agreement and patiently listen for a new revision. This is what disputants seek a mediator for – to *patiently* help them to do what they were not able to do alone. Most disputants fail to resolve their problems because they rush and fear the perceptions of others.

Stepping Into the Disputants' Shoes

Recall first an experience that you have had when someone listened to you, but it was obvious that they cared very little about your feelings. Possibly, we all are able to call up any number of instant memories in a variety of situations in which others appear to listen to us, but do not show us that they completely understand, empathize, or identify with what we (in that moment) are experiencing.

We will define the terms of listening in this chapter, but it is important to first distinguish how a person who is not listened to *feels*. As a mediator, to truly help the disputants you must imagine how it felt to "walk in their shoes." To understand what each side felt like as they went through this conflict is a good definition of **empathy** (as it is used in mediation). Showing empathy while you listen will help you respond with kindness. As a mediator, the ability to show kindness goes a long way toward stimulating the disputants to work together collaboratively.

Will The Person I Talk to *Empathize*

One of the best ways a mediator can learn to empathize is to envision himself in similar situations to the disputant. The disputants' situation and feelings will be different, but it is a helpful exercise. Compare the following every day scenarios to situations in your own life.

Your Experiences With Empathy

Imagine a recent experience in a "drive-thru" food restaurant in which you had a question about something or a specific need for your "order." How did the service person treat you? Did you feel understood, cared about, or appreciated? Compare the feelings you imagined with how a *caller* might feel when making first contact with your mediation office.

Now imagine taking back an item to a department store. You do not have your receipt and must explain why. Did the person take the time to understand your situation? How did you feel when they did (or did not understand)? Compare this to how a potential mediation client may feel if they have told you something that was hard to explain in an initial conversation.

Imagine making request at a restaurant to hold a gathering there. How did the person that you spoke with treat you? Did they empathize or make you feel uncomfortable? How about a situation of being invited to a large family reunion of distant relatives that you have not seen in some time, will you be met with understanding? Compare this to how a mediation client may feel upon seeing the "other" party in their dispute in their first mediation setting.

Finally, imagine that you must reveal the most embarrassing collection of information about yourself to a perfect stranger and simultaneously ask for his help. How do you feel? Are you scared? What will the stranger say? Will he judge you? How will you defend your mistakes? The comparison here is obvious. A client will experience all of the feelings and questions above before, during, and after his time spent with you in mediation.

All of these questions and more are included in the anxieties that disputants have and hope you understand before coming to talk to you and expecting you to listen.

Your Reponses As a Mediator

How will you respond? Will you take the time to understand disputants' worst mistakes from their perspective? How will you validate them for the things they did right? How will you gently and patiently confront them on the things they did wrong? Will you expect the conversation to get emotional, difficult, confusing, embarrassing, and awkward? It will.

If you deliver kind, caring, and empathetic responses to your disputants, you can expect it to. This (to me) is a good sign that you are doing your job well. You will be one-step further toward a better reaction to difficult statements if you go *in* (to the listening/responding experience) expecting the road to be rocky before it gets smooth. No one can ever react perfectly to every situation posed him in the exact moment it is posed.

It "counts" if you recognize a *reaction mistake* and correct it the next time you have an opportunity. A **reaction mistake** is measured in the response from the disputant. If the disputant's face becomes pained or he voices disapproval or disagreement with your reaction, you may then assess that you need to react in a kinder manner to this topic. It is likely that the topic is causing him more pain than you anticipated. Take a moment and gently ask if you understood; this should clear the misunderstanding.

It matters if you are patient and kind. It is all right to ask questions gently and with caring. Image that it is *you* that is telling the same tale that you are hearing. No one can completely know how another expects to be responded to in order to feel understood, but we can all convey kindness and understanding.

This is what every disputant will expect of you. As the mediator, *your* ego must go "out the window" in sacrifice of their need for someone to understand, to care, and to share with them for a little while – their pain, disappointment, anger, embarrassment, guilt, and sadness. Disputants, above all need the *best* of your ability as a mediator to deliver the skills defined below. Do your best. If you fail, begin again.

Two Essential Listening Skills

Here are some essential principles of how to listen, excerpted and paraphrased from Susie Michelle Cortright's (2008) 10 Tips to Effective & Active Listening Skills:

1. **Focus solely on what the speaker is saying**. Try not to think about what you are going to say next. The conversation will follow a logical flow after the speaker makes his point…

2. **Minimize internal distractions.** If your own thoughts keep horning in, simply let them go and continuously re-focus your attention on the speaker."

Eye Contact

Looking individuals in the eye with a kind expression conveys instantly that the speaker has your attention. **As a mediator, you need to maintain eye contact,** to the degree that you and the disputants are comfortable. If the disputants appear to feel uncomfortable with constant eye contact, then periodically focus on areas close to their face, but *away* from direct eye contact.

Stay focused on each disputant's facial area throughout the mediation process and do make direct eye contact in a kind manner periodically throughout mediation. Mediation is a business transaction as well as a session of listening; the disputants need their professional to keep them focused on the business at hand. Their objective is to reach an equitable agreement that respects them both if at all possible.

Facial Expression

As a mediator, your facial expressions need to reflect a degree of dramatic animation. Do not let your face remain stoic in reaction to extremely volatile information – good or bad. Show the disputants with your facial expression that you are listening. In a very genuine manner, listen to the stories disputants tell you and let your eyes, eyebrows, mouth, and entire face reflect that you are listening. You do not need to be overdramatic to convey that you are genuinely interested in what they need to tell you.

Posture

Your posture very clearly reflects whether your facial expressions are indeed genuine. A professional who is listening shows very clear body posturing – moving his body *toward* the speaker. **Face the person speaking.** Lean forward slightly to show you are paying attention.
You may also show your attention by turning both shoulders/ upper body toward the speaker while you are working at a dry-erase board, laptop or other tool of mediation. Even if you have to turn away, be aware of your body when you do so and be aware that you are turned away while you are writing or collecting material.

Remember to turn back and refocus immediately on the speaker in a kind manner as soon as you are able. The speaker will unconsciously be aware that you did this and will further unconsciously appreciate this gesture.

Open & Closed Body Positions

There are two types of body positions that are important to be familiar with because they are used so often to describe the both the physical and *figurative* "position" that the listener is reflecting.

An **open** body position indicates that a person is emotionally "open" or receptive to new ideas and information. Open body positions look "open." Arms and legs are open (not crossed) and a person's body is often turned toward the person speaking. Facial expressions reflect more open or upward brows and more receptive mouth position (nearer to a smile). Sometimes, arms or legs (one or the other) can be slightly crossed and the person can still be in an open position or in the process of transitioning to an open position. Open body positions further indicate that the listener is "open" to new concepts. It notes to the speaker unconsciously that the listener will accept was he has to say.

A **closed** body position indicates that a person is emotionally "closed" to receiving new information and ideas. Closed body positions likewise, look "closed." Arms and legs are usually crossed and a person's body is turned away from the person speaking.. Facial expressions reflect downwardly cast brows and a less receptive mouth position (nearer to a frown). Sometimes, arms or legs (one or the other set) are not crossed, but the body overall reflects disagreement and a "positioning" away from the person speaking. Closed body positions further indicate that the listener is "closed" *figuratively* to new concepts. It notes to the speaker unconsciously that the listener will not accept was he has to say.

Here is an acronym for body posturing that may further assist you to remember the qualities of good posture while attentively listening:

TABLE 3   **Five Steps for Attentive Listening**

"S.O.L.E.R.

Five steps to attentive listening:

S - **squarely** face the person
O - **open** your posture
L - **lean** towards the sender
E - **eye** contact maintained
R - **relax** while attending"

(Listening Skills, 2008, p.1)

Mirroring

While you are seated and listening to the person speaking, assure that you very slowly begin to mirror their body movements. **Mirroring** is the act of imitating body movements, as if looking at the person (speaking) in a mirror.

Your movements of body (as the mediator) should be a "mirror" reflection of the other person. If they cross their left leg over right, you would cross your leg (right over left to form the mirror). You would move your body in the same direction as you are seeing them move theirs. Practitioners will find that if they begin to pay attention to themselves, they may automatically mirror others without realizing this. After any professional practices this movement for a while, they will begin to do this instinctively.

It is important to pay attention to your body's movements and mirror the person who is speaking. When you mirror a speaker, you let them know non-verbally, that you are "with" them – or that you understand them and are "on their side." Disputants need this; they are describing very emotional problems, and they need non-verbal affirmation as well as verbal support that the professional involved cares.

As a mediator, you are in essence on "both sides." You must mirror both sides equally. You must listen without bias to both sides equally. Initially, this may seem "phony" to you as a new practitioner, and it is not a technique that you tell disputants you are doing, because they may feel that you are being disingenuous. However, the techniques of listening are designed to help both disputants, and when implemented with care assist the disputants to relax. You are there to help them both simultaneously. To help, you must use skilled techniques that have been proven to empower disputants to work through difficult issues.

Keep the Dialogue Flowing

Keeping the dialogue flowing in mediation is as important as keeping the gas flowing in an automobile on the highway. Never let yourself forget that mediation is also a business meeting (Doyle & Straus, 1976). Breaks are needed when individuals are talking about emotional conflicts, but when disputants return from breaks, it is the mediator's responsibility to keep the dialogue flowing and focused.
To do this, ask **questions for clarification** when the speaker is finished. As the mediator, your job is to obtain as much information as

possible. If you interrupt a disputants' train of thought, you may miss important information. To keep the conversation flowing, "say phrases such as "I wasn't aware of that," "tell me more…" [with genuine intention]. You may also use prompts that are more direct: *"What did you do then?"* and *"What did she actually use?"*

Do not Judge or Give Advisement

The biggest pitfall a mediator can make is giving advisement to disputants on how to solve the problems brought to mediation. I have seen new mediators write website blogs about how to give advice to disputants in mediation. In my experience, giving advice is a mistake. A friend can be sought for advice. Advice from a friend will be biased, but nonetheless; people often seek advice from friends.
Disputants seek professional skilled service from a mediator, not advice. Disputants often ask for advice because they are stuck. Effective mediation helps them to solve their own problem, which is more effective than any advice given.

Giving advisement to disputants is not a practice of mediation. Careful too that you do not begin to judge disputants' problems without recognizing this behavior in yourself.
Assure that as soon as the urge to judge or advice arises in you, you become aware of this feeling and refocus your listening skills and responses in a neutral and empathetic understanding. Here are some listening tips:

- **Avoid letting the speaker know how you handled a similar situation.** Unless they specifically ask for advice, assume they just need to talk it out.

- **Keep an open mind.** Wait until the speaker is finished before deciding that you disagree. Try not to make assumptions about what the speaker is thinking.

- **Even if the speaker is launching a complaint against you, wait until they finish to defend yourself.** The speaker will feel as though their point had been made. They won't feel the need to repeat it, and you'll know the whole argument before you respond.

Listening From a Caring Perspective: Empathy & Compassion

Conveying *empathy* is one of the most challenging components of active listening, yet without it, a disputant will not feel listened to. Likewise, to convey a sense of authentic *compassion* (to both parties equally) reflects the founding principles of mediation.

Empathy is a feeling of mutual understanding of emotion *and* experience. It is also the ability to communicate understanding. By definition, a situation that requires *empathy* to understand is one in which difficulty has been experienced. Individuals in dispute are in need of empathy from the moment they call you on the phone to request information. Think back to our section on "walking in the other person's shoes."

We all need others to empathize with us, even in the simplest situations. Though we may not verbalize it, we all need empathy and well all seek empathy. Often, our need of empathy is unconscious, but when we experience empathy from someone, it is always a welcome occurrence. When humans are in conflict, they both need and expect empathy from others. The problem is they seldom get empathy from others and this intensifies conflict.

The Expectation of Empathy

When individuals seek a mediator for help resolving a dispute, they expect empathy. To **empathize** with someone, the mediator must imagine that he is actually experiencing the situation the person is describing and give reactions that will be appreciated and thereby stimulate the process of healing.
If disputants do not get empathy, they leave the process, either physically (by not returning to the mediation table) or emotionally by "checking out". They will cease to challenge themselves to open their minds and not allow themselves to become vulnerable so they may consider new alternatives.
The mediated agreement then will not be realized and/or it will not be sustainable. Because the disputants will not emotionally connect with the mediator and thereby will not invest themselves into the process.

Stimulating the Opposing Side to Empathize

No matter how unlikely or unappealing the situation is to the mediator, to imagine that this situation is happening to *you* will help the opposing side *begin* to imagine their rival's experience.
To stimulate the opposing party to truly imagine the other side's experience and empathize with how the other side feels *begins* a process of *transforma-*

tion within the disputants. The field of transformative mediation is focused solely on the attainment of such an accomplishment. In any mediation, there exists the possibility of moments of empathy. These moments can exist separately or build on one another to for a new level of awareness.

Compassion

The embodiment of compassion is familiar to professionals in the helping professions. To convey compassion in mediation is to show caring to both sides equally about issues of loss and disappointment. It is a part of the listening process that should not be overlooked because it is another stimulant to the healing and recovery process for the disputant.

To fail to show compassion to an individual, regardless of what type of conflict situation is described is an error. Disputants expect mediators to show compassion. Disputants look for the level of compassion that they can expect from the mediator on the *first* occasion that they either speak to you or meet you.

Showing **compassion** means to reflect in your facial expressions, verbal statements, and body posturing that you care about the difficult situation that is being described to you by the speaker. In showing these behaviors mentioned above, your statements should agree with the speaker's statements and not point out the opposite view point.

For instance, if the speaker states, "I hate it when someone yells at me in traffic for not going fast enough; it stresses me out." A compassionate mediator statement in response should be, "I know; I hate that too." A non-compassionate response would be, "You shouldn't feel stressed out; you should ignore them." This latter statement negates the initial feeling expressed by the speaker and does not convey compassion.

In mediation, the absence of compassion conveys a lack of caring and respect. When a disputant returns to these negative feelings, he is more likely to become combative. You may feel yourself intelligent by playing "devil's advocate" to points raised that you see the opposite view of, but you will not help your disputants by taking this perspective. Allow the disputants to discover these alternate perspectives on their own and they will embrace opposite viewpoints with their own loyalty.

As a mediator, when you convey compassion, you free the disputant to discover his own lessons and view points that apply to his situation. You further create an atmosphere of empowerment that will enable the disputant to work through his own obstacles after completing mediation.

Chapter 6

...The Lord came and stood there, calling as the other times. Samuel! Samuel! And Samuel said, speak, for your servant is listening.

- I Samuel 3:9-10

Active Listening: The Heart & Soul of Mediation

To listen with active participation is the heart and soul of mediation. The skills of active listening have been around for many decades. They serve as a method for both understanding and delivering skilled listening to individuals seeking professional help for just that purpose.

To be able to carry out each one of these skills with ease takes time and practice, but is essential for the mediator. Mediators are required to have the highest skill attainment of listening, because the one sentence a mediator "gets" to make while listening, must be composed of several of these concepts simultaneously.

Active versus Passive Listening

A distinction between "active" listening and "passive" listening is necessary for the attainment of active listening skills, as these definitions guide the delivery of listening technique. **Passive listening** occurs when one individual (the 1st person) is *present* when someone else (the 2nd person) is talking, but there is no *evidence* that the 1st person (passive listener) is listening.
An outsider looking at a conversation (with a passive listener) could not tell (by appearance, body position, facial expression, response, or lack thereof) if the 1st person had heard, what the 2nd person had. An example of passive listening occurs in a conversation in an automobile. The 1st person is

driving a car and speaking while the passenger (2nd person) sits motionless. The second person in the above scenario is exhibiting passive listening. In this actual situation, it is difficult to show active listening, but the physical appearance of the passenger reflects the exact same body posturing and lack of responses show in a passive listener.

Active listening occurs when one individual (1st person) shows through his behavior that he is listening to the other individual (2nd person). The first person makes eye contact, nods, and asks specific questions that indicate that he (1st person) is actively listening to the other person (2nd person). The concepts, questions, and statements that reflect active listening are detailed below.

The Statements of Active Listening

Asking Questions for Clarification

Asking questions for clarification can be one of the easiest aspects of mediation. The more questions you ask, especially when you ask them in a kind, supportive and non-invasive manner, the more everyone in the mediation process will learn to create a resolution.

Clarifying

To clarify points made by a disputant, the mediator asks very specific questions of the speaker. The goal is to move the speaker from a broad generalization to a specific point you can work with.

For example, the disputant states, *I was so mad when he told me about it that I screamed at my child. I probably doomed our daughter to counseling in later life.* The mediator would clarify by slowly asking any one of the following questions:

> ✓ "Let me see if I understand what you were mad about, was it a cell phone bill? **Yes**

> ✓ Was it Jane's cell phone? **Yes**
> ✓ Did you talk to her about it? **Yes**
> ✓ When did that conversation occur?   **Yesterday**
> ✓ Have you talked with her since?"   **No**

Asking these questions slowly and *gently* helps a disputant to begin to see the larger problem. He also begins to realize that this problem has workable parts that can be improved.

To clarify these points also serves to focus the discussion *on* the specific goal that this mediation has for this problem. It serves to clarify issues into manageable components for the disputant, so that their problems do not feel overwhelming.

It is a good practice to ask very specific questions like this about the issues of greatest important to the disputants. It is likely that the issues of greatest importance may also be the issues that cause the disputants the most confusion. Utilize closed questions and limit open-ended questions when clarifying to keep clients focused on understanding the issues.

Slow gentle questioning assists disputants to begin to compartmentalize issues of confusion into issues that they can continue to work on when they leave mediation meetings.

A final benefit of clarifying points comes from the information provided by the disputants. The information gleaned guides the development of the resolution.

Responses of Active Listening

Check-Out

A **check-out** in active listening skills means to literally "check-out" whether you heard the person correctly. The mediator would specifically ask the speaker, "did I understand you to say that *(this)*_____was *(that)* _____....?"

This simple active listening skill (when delivered with gentle caring) serves to correct misconceptions, and models the same behavior for the opposing disputant. It makes excellent use of mediation time toward the resolution, and helps prevent wasted mediation time in pursuit of incorrect assumptions. Disputants pay high fees for mediation. If you, the mediator understand the disputant *in*correctly, you will likely pursue an **incorrect analysis.** You may waste precious mediation time with questions and responses about the wrong concept.

It is best to check-out each and every small fact that you are unsure of as soon as the information conveyed becomes confusing to you. By doing so, you further create an important precedent for the mediation. You set up a safe environment for anyone in the mediation to "check-out" the information being conveyed.

The "Check-out" a Mediation Technique for Discovery

The check-out is a powerful tool for disputants to discover causes for their dispute. When disputants begin to understand why something started, they learn how they can use their own ability and resources to resolve the problem. Once they realize that "checking something out" is simple and a good practice, they feel empowered to get more information about their dispute in a respectful manner. Giving disputants the message that "checking something out" is okay and in fact, a good thing to do provides them a new coping skill for resolving conflict both now and in the future.

When someone "check's out" information, he may frequently discover that he did in fact understand the information incorrectly in the *past* and may discover one reason the dispute originated in the first place. Often, disputes begin and worsen because of a *lack* of specific information or correct information. To use the "check-out" as a technique of mediation, allows disputants to discreetly discover an error they may have made in the conflict.

If they are then allowed time to process this information in an atmosphere of caring and understanding, the conflict may (and often does) slowly unravel into more smooth understandings and communication.

A new, more accurate understanding of information may change the perceptions of both disputants about their disagreement. A change in perception greatly benefits the mediation discussion and resolution.

Summarizing

Summarizing what a speaker is saying keeps both you and the speaker "on the same page." To **summarize**, the listener restates everything that he has heard using as many of the exact words and phrases that the speaker used as possible. In pure summarization, the listener would refrain from using their own words and interpretations of what the listener as heard .

A listener should summarize what he has heard after every five to ten sentences, depending on the *gravity* of the information (how heavily filled with emotion) and *intensity* of the information (how much detailed information is in one sentence.

For instance, if a person conveys extreme emotion and very detailed information, the listener will want to summarize what has heard as often as possible in a conversation. The listener will want to check for clarity and understanding of exact information conveyed. A misunderstanding may greatly affect the resolution of a conflict and can be cleared up with an accurate summary.

Summarize highly emotional information often. It gives the speaker a moment to breathe and assures that you understand. Emotional concepts are often vague. Summarize long lists of detail often, to assure that you have understood all elements relayed. Information that is not as emotional or packed with detail may be summarized a little less often, depending on the ability of the speaker to convey his thoughts.

Most speakers have extreme difficulty conveying emotional information and have difficulty conveying information that confuses them. Therefore, as a listener, **when you summarize what you have heard, you help the speaker to both convey this information better, and understand the confusing information with more clarity**.

Summarizing for Clarification (Emotional Content)

To **summarize for clarification**, the listener gently interrupts the speaker and quickly summarizes what he has heard. This active listening skill can serve two functions. It allows the mediator to clarify a small chunk of information and it serves to re-focus the speaker.

This type of summarizing allows the speaker to take a brief break, while he listens to you. These small moments of "break" (from speaking) for the speaker allows him or her to absorb that someone else in the room is creating a safe place for him to talk. It is important for the listener to take great care in his summarization when the speaker has been very sad or upset.

Creating this safe place of focus and supportive attention to the speaker's needs greatly helps an emotional speaker to become calmer and feel more empowered. **Empowerment** enables the speaker to feel as if he has the ability to not only talk about this conflict, but also find resolution.

Summary Response

A **summary response** is a singular statement that sums up several facts that have been difficult for the speaker to state. For example, the speaker states:

"…I had a car wreck… then I lost my job….the bills got out of control… I did not know what to do about bankruptcy…the attorney seemed trustworthy…"

The mediator, in summary response could state, "So after the wreck, you lost your job and your ability to pay your bills. The attorney suggested bankruptcy, and he seemed trustworthy?" These two summary statements do not interject any new words, judgments, or framing by the mediator. These statements simply serve to summarize a collection of facts with the purpose of assisting the disputant to feel empowered to talk about a very difficult set of circumstances.

Responses of Reflective Listening

Reflective listening takes the concept of *active* listening a step further. When a mediator **reflectively listens** to a speaker, he interjects his own analysis of what he has heard and *reflects* this back to the speaker in a statement or response.

Reflective listening further incorporates the listener's *perception* of the feelings experienced by the speaker. **The listener would simply add in his *own* impression of how this information made the speaker *feel*.** This more advanced active listening skill is used when disputants are avoiding their emotions and omitting how the issues within the dispute have upset them. Disputes are by nature upsetting. To omit these emotions greatly hinders the discovery of an effective and lasting resolution. If disputants *are* conveying how they feel, then a mediator would *not* use reflective listening techniques.

Reflective Response

The **reflective response** is a statement made by a professional listener that allows the listener to interject the *listener's* perceptions (using the listener's own words) of what he had just heard.

Here is an example:
The speaker states, "After work, nothing happened…when the car engine blew, I just stopped talking to him. If he wasn't going to listen to me about putting oil in a car … I just stopped."
The mediator makes the following reflective response question just after hearing the speaker: "I'm confused, let me try to state what I think you

were trying to say. …After the car engine blew, you were so angry that you stopped talking to your husband. You felt that if he would not listen to you about oil, he wouldn't listen to you about how *you* felt about him ignoring you when he came home from work?"

The mediator would as simply as possible restate his interpretation of the information heard, as well as the feelings he felt that the speaker conveyed.

Delivering Reflective Responses

The mediator's perspective will likely be *slightly* inaccurate, and the speaker will re-define their meaning for everyone listening. This active listening skill serves as an initial method (in the mediation process) of introducing the idea that *another* perception of the speaker's story exists.

This act of delivering a reflective response should be done *only* when a strong rapport between the disputants and mediator has been established. In addition, the mediator would need to have created a very safe atmosphere of caring empathetic responses first, so that disputants understand that his questions are entirely objective and not biased.

The reflective response can initiate a subtle exploration of new points of view and stimulate new options for consideration. *Reflective response should be used in moderation. It is further important that the mediator **conveys very simple and respectful reflective responses,** to role model this behavior for the opposing side.

Paraphrasing

Paraphrasing is a commonly used active listening skill. To paraphrase means simply to "re-phrase" what you have heard. Another definition of paraphrasing is to re-state a message using fewer words that get more to the point.

Paraphrasing is used by highly skilled mediators and counselors. It is actually a bit "dangerous" to paraphrase. Paraphrasing can influence both the disputant and the opposing side toward a different perspective. In essence – this is the height of the "directive" style of mediation (see chapter seven).

Paraphrasing is implemented in a very *subtle* manner and often it is *unconsciously* done by the mediator. It is important for mediators to be conscious of paraphrasing. When a neutral professional paraphrase's, **he puts his *own* spin on the information received and conveyed.** Some very highly skilled mediators use paraphrasing to introduce the possibility of a new perspective.

This technique should be used with caution, if ever chosen. Mediators should avoid exerting their influence over the resolution process, toward objectives created by the *mediator*.

Using Paraphrasing Within Several Active Listening Techniques

Paraphrasing can be embedded within the technique of "reflective summary" or "reflective response." Some mediators may use paraphrasing when they "check-out" information or give a straight "summary" of information as well. It is important to use exact words instead of paraphrasing whenever possible and especially when clarifying information.

A mediator, with pure, neutral focus can do an excellent job of paraphrasing. Neutrality is *essential* to paraphrasing; otherwise, the mediation can become biased in an instant. **For the mediator, recovering from a perception of bias by one side or the other is nearly impossible.**

Here is a *good* example of paraphrasing: The Disputant says, "She nags me about visitation constantly, and it makes me mad." Mediator paraphrases, "so you wish to request your wife to not ask you questions repeatedly about the visitation schedule?"

This statement encompasses several active listening concepts: **paraphrasing, checking-out** (for accuracy) and **reflective response** (one response). It further serves to "**reframe**" the discussion (see the section below). Here is where the *influence* of the paraphrase comes in. The mediator chose to influence the discussion by paraphrasing the "slur" of "she nags" into a request and directed the conversation toward a specific goal – of resolving the visitation issue.

This singular statement served all of these purposes for the disputants in the mediation. It was a bit of a "reach" on the part of the mediator – imposing his more positive "spin" on the emotionally charged statement made. In this instance, it is likely to help move the disputants toward resolution. If the issue of "nagging" needed further attention (as opposed to a simple reframe), the disputants will bring it back up again.

Reflective Summation

A reflective summation is used by the mediator to summarize what he has heard using his own perceptions to describe the information. A reflective summation further describes the listener's perception of how the speaker feels about the information shared. When a mediator uses a reflective summation, a "check-out" for accuracy and response by the speaker is stated.

Here is an example:

> The disputant says, "I love Joey and Jane, but their friends are another matter. They are disrespectful to me, and I cannot stand being around them."

> "Let me see if I understand. You said that you love your children and that they are very important to you. At the same time, you cannot stand being with their friends. Is that what you are saying?"

The mediator/listener in this example has both "checked-out" the information he heard and summarized the information as well. He did so in the form of a question, allowing the speaker to correct or clarify the information heard or the perspective expressed. When a mediator uses the exact words of the speaker, this becomes easy and most conducive to maintaining a good discussion.

Framing/Re-Framing

Framing is the manner in which a mediator re-states a presented issue to reflect a *new perspective* of the information. Mediators are able to frame an issue when he summarizes or restates a set of statements to assure accuracy. In the example above the mediator took the additional step of presenting the information in the same manner that it was presented by the original speaker.

Any perspective may be conveyed in framing. Positive *or* negative perspectives can be conveyed to promote a more specific discussion. For instance, "Sally's" perspective may be conveyed in contrast to "Joe's" perspective. Also, the perspective of an outside family member may be presented (their child's perspective) to frame another way to look a specific point of contention.

The mediation discussion can be *framed* to begin the day's interactions. For example, when the mediation is framed as a family cooperative effort (focused in the best needs of the entire family) the use of "framing" serves to influence the disputants to consider not only their own feelings, but also the possible perspective of the other family members.

An example of this type of framing would be:
Mediator opening statement for the second day of "child custody mediation":
"We are here today to create a visitation schedule that will indeed respect all
individuals involved. We have established that maintaining Sally's best interests are a priority of both sides. Since we agree on this first priority, let's
find a second point of agreement."

This statement *frames* the work for that day or segment of mediation. By
framing the work this positive, cooperative manner, the mediator creates an
atmosphere of collaboration for resolving the mutual goal of "setting up a
consistent visitation schedule" in the best interests of "Sally."

The mediator's choice to do this will influence the mediation. This is the
objective of positive framing. Small agreements framed in an atmosphere of
collaboration will assist disputants successfully discuss more difficult issues
later in mediation.

Re-Framing

Re-Framing is the act of re-stating a negatively presented issue in a different and more objective manner. Most re-frames are also attempts to re-state
information in a positive manner. To re-state (or reframe) an issue negatively would serve little point in mediation, unless this was done as an exercise
in **role-reversal,** assuming the "role" – thoughts, feelings, statements, opinions, and ideas of the opposing side.

Reframing is most often used to change the direction the mediation is head-
ed (if disputants become combative or the discussion becomes less
productive or abusive).

An example of reframing (when a disputant curses) would be:

*"John will pay ALL of the damn child support on time." The mediator may
re-frame this statement as: "I understand that cursing is something you find
"normal," and is a part of your everyday life. Would it be acceptable to you
if I modified your statement to just read – John will pay all of the child support on time?"*

This "reframe" serves as a reflective response and check-out. To reframe the
demand and curse words serves to respect everyone involved. Later, disputants will be glad that negative slams were not included in the writing down

of a brainstormed idea. The mediator honored the disputants' request, but reframed the question with a "check-out" in his last sentence.

Final Summary

The **final summary** offers the opportunity for the mediator to present the all the information he has heard to check accuracy.

For example, a disputant may state:
> "He yelled at me as soon as I brought up the issue of buying clothing. I hate it when he does this without even giving me the chance to explain. Our arguments were always about money, but mostly we argued about the clothes I bought. I needed clothes just like he needed parts for his car."

A mediator may summarize this statement by saying:

> "So you argued about money and mostly about the clothes you bought with your money. Your husband yelled at you as soon as you brought up buying clothing, and you hated this. Did I summarize what you've told me correctly?"

This is an example of a straight summarization (without reflecting the feelings or paraphrasing any of the material that you heard with your perceptions of how the speaker feels).

Here are some important facts to remember about summarizing:

A good final summary pulls together, organizes and integrates the major aspects of the dialogue that the listener hears. A summary does not add new information and it does not add new ideas.

Here are two different ways to begin a final summary:

> 1 - *Let's take a few minutes to go over [your ideas] and write them on the board…*

> 2- *The three major points that you've talked about are…*

Transitioning & Other Skills of Verbal Interaction

One of the final active listening skills is transitioning. To **transition** from pure listening to the introduction of new information is important in mediation. The mediator may need to introduce a new concept that may *not* be in agreement with one or both disputants. To introduce the new information, the mediator must create a bridge (transition) between his listening responses to his more active role in leading the mediation.

Before you introduce information that is not in agreement with what the other person said, you must use a "transition sentence" to bridge to prepare disputants for a different set of reactions. A **transition sentence provides support** for the disputant's point of view **without necessarily agreeing with it**, and at the same time, makes the disputant receptive to a different point of view.

There are two parts **to a transition sentence:**

1. Statement that supports the current view (without agreeing)
2. Announcement that new information is coming,"

For example:
The disputant states, "It makes me mad! I hate having to wait to pay my bills!"
The mediator replies: "So you were angry at having to wait each month to pay bills, but is it possible that there was a reason unknown to you that money was withheld?"

The mediator used a reflective summation phrase in the first part of the transition sentence that bridged specific information into the latter part of the sentence that introduced new information with a question.

Transition Sentences

One of the most common places a mediator uses a transition sentence is in a caucus. A caucus occurs when the disputants meet with the mediator separately in a private room to discuss a specific issue.

Here is an Example of a Transition Sentence in a caucus:
The disputant states, "he did not show up to meet with me, so I know he really does not care. He is lying to you in our discussions."

The mediator replies, "That is an interesting point…I can see how you could have that opinion. What if the information you had was not accurate? If the other side had another meeting time that was different from yours, then that may explain why he did not show up. Let me request clarification of this issue from the other party."

In this instance, the mediator reflects empathy, and then introduces the possibility of new information or a different perspective. He further requests to clarify the information with the other side to see if a change in position from the other perspective is possible. This technique is often used in directive court mediation to work through difficult issues in a very step-by-step manner.

Transitioning Between Mediation Steps

Another instance that may require a transition sentence comes near the end of the first portion of mediation. As you close the "brainstorming" portion of mediation. You may use a transition sentence to carry the disputant from the first half of mediation to the next stage.
For example:
> "You have worked through this issue for a considerable amount of time, and the work you have done may have been what was needed to assist you to consider the new options. Jane suggested "this" sentence and John suggested "that" sentence. Would either of these options work for your visitation schedule?"

In these sentences, the mediator used the ideas created in brainstorming to transition from "brainstorming" *to* writing the first draft of an agreement. He established the introduction of new material *and* began a new phase of the mediation *based on* the work that had already been accepted. This is a "big picture" use of the concept of transitioning; the mediator transitioned from the initial phases of mediation to the final phase of mediation. Many of these concepts resemble one another and may appear confusing upon first read, but in the context of providing mediation, the use of these techniques becomes easier. The most challenging of the techniques of mediation is confrontation.

Confrontation

To **confront** a speaker, the listener challenges what has been said by questioning the accuracy of the speaker's opinions. Confrontation is a difficult process for every mediator; for it places into question the mediator's loyalty (from the disputant's perspective) and neutrality.

Confrontation is best started in the middle of the mediation process. To confront disputants at the beginning of the mediation will damage the rapport between the mediator and both disputants. The **rapport** is the state of trust between the mediator and disputants. A good rapport needs to be well established and maintained throughout any instance of confrontation.

At some point in any effective mediation, the mediator will need to confront both disputants equally. If a good rapport has been established (using the attentive skills and active listening skills detailed above) then the transition from listening and empowerment to gentle confrontation will remain in tact.

The Characteristics of Good Listening & Responding

In a discussion, the mediator must reflect that he is listening and simultaneously stimulate the disputant to continue to work toward the positive goals set. The mediator must also continue to focus the disputants as they share broad sets of information about these problems *and* the emotions that are associated with them. It is an extremely challenging task to do well.
The consequences are high for the disputants and the outcome of mediation extraordinarily important to all involved. This is why complete mastery and delivery of these listening skills is so important. Practice much before you begin to carry out these skills of listening on your own.

Emotional Healing: Mediation versus Counseling

In the course of mediation, deep emotions are brought up and must be dealt with. It is important to note however, that a prolonged discussion of emotional content is not appropriate for the mediation setting. Disputants often report that they have *personally* benefited from some emotional healing because of a good mediation, but this is not the objective of mediation. In counseling – the objective is to enhance functioning in one's *personal* life. In mediation – the objective is to stimulate disputants to find a resolution to several interrelated problems and draft the resolution into an agreement that two parties will maintain over time.

The energy required to resolve the problems presented into an agreement is great. Often, to resolve the issues presented *well* will stimulate a different kind of healing that comes with time as the disputants experience better relations with one another. The success of resolving a conflict with someone is quite powerful and is enough of an objective.

Mediators use their ability to subtly *stimulate* and *reinforce* healing by giving validation to choices that will promote positive growth. In this way, mediators are able to plant tiny seeds, when the opportunity presents itself. The goal in mediation is to stay focused on resolving the dispute and writing an agreement, not resolve the many levels of deep feeling that will arise. If the disputants experience negative feelings repeatedly in mediation, the mediator would simply listen, caringly, but not respond as a counselor. He would take a break allow for some recovery and continue to assist the disputants to focus back on their dispute.

How Long to Allow for Emotional Release

The appropriate length of the discussion of emotional content will vary by mediation, but in general, you should look to the other party's reactions as a guide. If the other party is showing extreme frustration with a lengthy pursuit of emotional sharing (passed ½ hour) then consider patiently and kindly changing the discussion.

For instance, if the topic begins at 8:00am as: '*the pain one side felt after the initial discussion of the divorce,*' the mediator should allow for a respectful amount of time to discuss how this issue affected *both* sides equally. After a respectful time has passed, then consider asking how the other side feels about this in a kind and facilitative manner. Remain focused on mediation goals.

All responses should reference the goals of mediation, framing information toward work to obtain mediation objectives. After an hour of emotional sharing on one topic, it is time to re-focus disputants back onto the business of resolution. It is fine to return to emotional sharing later for brief periods, as these times of emotional release may greatly benefit the completion of a more holistic and lasting resolution. However, emotional counseling is not the goal or objective of mediation.

If the disputants fail to reach an agreement because you allow them to take you (the professional) down too many tangential paths of emotional conflict, they will blame you if they do not reach an agreement. They will further fail to get holistic emotional healing as well – they will become further fragmented by the process.

Referrals to Counseling

After an emotional session, a gentle reference in private to how a specific counselor you know is best. Assure not to refer one side to counseling while the other side is present. As a professional, you must focus your skills on the goals of mediation, however, as a human being; you may see a need for this family and recognize how much help another professional could be to them. When you refer individuals and families who have serious problems to other professionals, you give those who come to see you the best service.

If they come to see you for mediation, provide *mediation* service not counseling. Disputants will respect you more for having the ability to limit their emotional sharing in the end, when you continue to accomplish small goals in the mediation process.

Refer disputants to a counseling professional that you have known for some time and trust. If you do not know a good professional counselor, then it is best to refer them to a fellow professional who has a well-established reputation for good service.

Chapter 7

Send forth Your light and Your truth; let them Guide me.

- Psalms 43:3

Styles of Mediation: Directive, Facilitative & Guided

The components of mediation *style* have been around since mediation theory was formulated into mediation practice in the early 1990's. However, within the practice of mediation, there is diversity within the traditions of style.

Styles of Mediation

The **style** of mediation that each individual mediator chooses is embodied in the way a mediator initiates interactions between the disputants. Each mediator chooses a style based on the type of conflict that he wishes to serve. For instance, court based mediation utilizes a more directive style whereas community based mediation uses a more facilitative style. Also, mediators choose a preferred style of mediation that best suits his background, personality, and prior experience with client service.

The traditional terms used to describe mediator style are the directive (or evaluative) approach and the facilitative approach. Some theorists categorize a third style of mediation as transformative.

Transformative mediation is a type of mediation that most often employs the use of the facilitative style. This distinction is explored in greater depth below. In actuality, all mediation is directive at some point, and to embrace the directive *skill* in a more accurate manner provides the most help to those seeking to provide mediation service. Below, the two most prevalent styles of mediation, directive and facilitative are compared.

The Directive Style of Mediation

The **directive** style of mediation provides great assistance to disputants seeking a skilled practitioner to settle issues of property. Indeed, a measure of direction is needed in each mediation. Disputants have exhausted all of their ideas for resolving their dispute and are often confused about both their problem and the mediation process. Clear, well-delivered direction can be of great comfort to someone seeking to resolve a conflict if the direction is delivered in a flexible manner that is patient with the process of discovering common needs and interests.

However, *over* directive mediators can remove or seriously diminish opportunities for healing and transformation. Even though directive mediation helps provide disputants pathways for resolution, a very directive approach does not promote an atmosphere of ease and good will. It often makes disputants feel uncomfortable and intimidated by the mediation process. Directive mediators are beneficial to disputes that require large amounts of negotiation (for financial settlement). The directive process assists those who are focusing solely on reaching property or financial agreement to find common ground.

Facilitative Style of Mediation

The other style of traditional mediation is called facilitative. **Facilitative** mediators *follow* where the disputants *lead* the resolution process. Facilitative mediators often apply leadership skills to their practice of mediation. This can be confusing for a new practitioner to understand, as both styles of professional mediation skill require leadership on the part of the mediator, just in different degrees.
Facilitative mediators are beneficial to disputants who themselves want to control the entire process; however, disputants do expect the facilitative mediator to be able to take more of a leadership position when the dispute becomes difficult.
It is important to know that all disputes have emotional conflicts embedded within them, and the facilitative style allows for more flexibility within the mediation procedure to deal with the emotional components. This

additional flexibility often creates an atmosphere more conducive to the *expression* of the many complex emotions that lie within all conflicts. For this reason, a strong trend toward the use of the "facilitative" style became prominent in the mid to late 1990's.

Mediators sought to create an atmosphere conducive to healing, but often faced the dilemma of how to assist disputants to resolve the many smaller conflicts that arose in such a process. Facilitative mediators must be highly skilled and trained in the more transformative mediation methods to use the pure facilitative approach. Conflicts become complicated quickly and require an efficient professional response in mediation.

Mediators frequently return to a gentle directive style when challenges arise from too many smaller conflicts simultaneously. Possibly, this term "facilitative" helped professionals (in the past) to distinguish between the two forms that were developing. This terminology (facilitative) benefited the more transformative mediations that were sought in small community outreach programs and in international mediations. Since the practice of mediation was still in a developmental state, the use of the most familiar terminology was relied upon.

The Guided Style of Mediation

Today, theses terms are outdated. The need for a style that incorporates the best of both styles is becoming clear. A third mediation style would more specifically serve those seeking domestic dispute mediations. The **Guided** Mediation Style is a new method theorized with this work that seeks to provide a style of mediation that better serves individuals, families, and groups seeking mediation.

To *guide* a set of disputants through the mediation process, the mediator *gently directs.* When each disputant is ready to express himself and actually begins to exhibit the actions (that are present in the next level of the mediation structure), the mediator is there to guide them *to* the next level. To conceptualize an enhanced form of both facilitative and directive mediation will deliver a more refined set of techniques for professional practice. The guided method simply provides a more specific set of protocols to the mediator. There is room for all three styles in the mediation field.

Understanding the Three Styles

The guided style of mediation lies on a continuum in the middle of the other two styles.

TABLE 4   **Styles & Types of Mediation**

Styles of Mediation

Directive_____Guided_____Facilitative

Types of Mediation

Court Based_____Goal Centered_____Transformative

Directive mediation would lie on one end and Facilitative mediation on the other. The Guided style of mediation would fall in the middle because of its use of at least ½ of the characteristics of the other styles. To compare the three <u>styles</u> of mediation to the <u>types</u> of mediation that each may be successfully applied to - helps to distinguish these concepts from one another.

Comparing the <u>Types</u> of Mediation to Styles

Court Based Mediation

Court Based mediation (as defined in this paradigm) focuses primarily on the resolution of disputes originated or destined for the court system. These disputes either began as a legal suit or will become a legal suit at some point. Mediation offers disputants in these cases the opportunity to more deeply explore complicating factors - outside of the call and response protocols of court. This type of mediation is best suited to a more directive style of mediation, as disputants benefit from a mediation format that will assist them to settle the issues in the conflict outside of court.

It is important for directive mediators to note the need to be open to the emotional aspects of dispute resolution. Court mediated disputes have emotional components too, and the resolution of these matters always requires patience and a more open set of responses from the mediator. The mediator must be prepared to be flexible at any time within the process to emotions that arise and give time and validation equally to both sides for the resolution of contentious issues. To do so, insures a more holistic and lasting resolution.

Transformative

Transformative mediation is different from court-based mediation; it uses a less directive style. In court mediation, a mediator might actually state out loud, "Susan, now you tell your side of the story, and we will listen and ask questions for clarification only." This is a directive statement. A more transformative mediation process often begins with storytelling – in a *non-directive* fashion. After the mediator describes the guidelines, the mediator would "facilitate" only by simply nodding his head to a disputant, to indicate that it was his turn.

The mediator would then ask questions for clarification and in the same manner, indicate (as non-verbally as possible) to the opposite side that is it their turn to tell their side of the story. Different cultures respond to less verbal direction. Some cultures would view directive statements as disrespectful of their cultural norms. In these instances, the transformative process works well for conflicts that are filled with deep emotions and/or problems of unknown origin. Conflicts evolve over time, and often many individuals do not understand why there are problems or what the problems are. Individuals may feel threatened or intimidated by too many directives and may shut down.

The facilitative style of mediation gives the disputant the freedom to discover what their most important issues are and affords them an opportunity to better define their problems. This approach creates an atmosphere conducive to the possibility of *transforming* their crisis into an opportunity for healing and growth.

Goal Centered

The **goal-centered** type of mediation (referred to in Table 4) is recommend-ed for mediation experiences that are not as easy to match a specific style to. Often, disputes come into the mediation process in a cloud of confusion. Disputants do not know what to do or how best to approach the resolution of their conflict.

When the initial mediation discussions begin (*defining the process and describing the roles of all involved*) disputants then are introduced to the concept of setting goals. If the goals of the dispute do not become clear, then a goal centered approach would best serve disputants to discover how best to resolve their conflict.

Since many mediations begin in this fashion, it is best for the mediator to take some time to learn as much about the needs of the disputants and assess which type and style of mediation may best serve the disputants' needs. **Goal centered mediation** is designed to assist disputants to better focus their energy and knowledge (of their own dispute) toward goals that will best help them arrive at a *mutually* beneficial agreement.

This type of mediation follows the work of psychological theory for goal-centered counseling. In this method, clients seek to discover the goals that each of the problems of their lives bring forth. The practitioner seeks to assist the client in discovering his own priorities for his issues and how these lead him to form the goals of resolution. The practitioner does not set the goals; the disputant creates his own goals.

Sometimes, the mediator does have to gently prompt the disputant with a phrase or simple statement, but the gentler the statement is, the more likely that the disputant will feel empowered rather than intimidated. This more gentle style of guiding the mediation serves to assist disputants (rather than leaving them confused about what they will be doing) while helping them to resolve their own conflict.

Disputant Expectations

All disputants wish to obtain at least a minimal measure of healing by going through the mediation process. Even the most directive mediation does eventually promote a small measure of healing when an agreement is reached. The process of opening issues in an atmosphere of acceptance and understanding immediately creates the foundation for healing.

The only time healing does not occur in mediation is when an unbalanced agreement is reached. If one side clearly dominates the agreement and the other sides' needs are not addressed, then the mediated agreement will not promote healing; it will provoke deeper conflict. It is never the expectation of the disputant to deepen his conflict, but is often the result of ineffective mediation.

Inadequately trained mediators, unfortunately promote poor resolutions that do not holistically address the problems embedded within each dispute. Every dispute has deeper issues of emotional conflict embedded within it. To deny this fact is to begin a process of poor resolution for a set of disputants. Frequently, disputants deny the existence of deeper emotional conflicts because they are in denial.

Embarrassment, pride, power imbalance and "saving face," all are reasons for this denial, and the denial by one or both sides often persists throughout the mediation process. Many disputants deny the emotional aspects of their conflict for years prior to and following mediation. A silent expectation of every disputant is for the mediator to create an atmosphere that is safe enough for the expression of deeper, painful issues to be carefully expressed and positively resolved.

As a mediator, to realize this expectation before the mediation begins is important to providing the best resolution that these disputants expect you to give them. Every mediation will be different; therefore every set of expectations and issues of contention different. Knowledge of another style of mediation to approach these differences with only enhances the professional's ability to provide the most effective service.

Disadvantages of "Bottom-Line" Mediation

One of the most prevalent trends of the 1980's, "bottom-line" thinking extends into present day professional analysis in many service industries. Condensing human stories into "bottom-line" summations became an overused technique that unfortunately permeated many types of professional practice.

"Bottom-line" focus eliminates the opportunity for the deeper and more important resolve of hurt. This unfortunate consequence has been realized in numerous conflicts, the most sensational of which was the MOVE crisis in Philadelphia. If the professionals involved had not sought to constantly focus on "bottom-line" news reports (and the effects of such on public opinion) but rather sent in mediators with a more open and caring style of mediation practice, the awful consequences of that series of conflicts could have been avoided.

Adapting the Existing Styles of Mediation

All three styles of mediation can assist disputants to better explore and re-solve their conflicts. To adapt the assessment process for mediation to include more specific styles (such as the guided method and goal-centered type of mediation) would help distinguish the best practices of mediation to address the disputes that are brought for assistance. Providing a disputant the most clarity and best possible method for resolution can be a comfort at a time when emotional confusion is high and knowledge of how to deal with it is nearly non-existent.

To both acknowledge and respect the confusion that is normally present in conflict , enables us to rise above the crisis's that enter all our lives and have the ability (long term) to prohibit us from succeeding. To adapt the existing styles of mediation into a method that helps *guide* disputants through the labyrinth of their feelings (during the resolution process) creates an atmos-phere for better dispute resolution.

Chapter 8

*As Apostles of Christ we could have
been a burden to you, but we were
gentle among you, like a mother
caring for her little children.*

- I Thessalonians 2:7

Mediation Skills: A Caring Approach

All of the skills that are required for secular mediation are required pastoral mediators as well. To be objective, non-biased, organized, and systematic in the approach one uses for mediation is vital to performing mediation service.

A Caring Approach

A good pastoral mediator should have patience, wisdom, experience (*in listening to many disputes over many years of time*) and the inclination to provide objective, spiritual guidance. He further must have the ability to apply an open mind to issues in dispute that may come into conflict with his own personal values. We will explore the concept of spiritual guidance for the pastoral mediator in this chapter.

Providing spiritual guidance is how a pastoral mediator is different from the secular mediator. One is not able to provide inspiration if one is fumbling with the "know-how" of mediation procedure and process. A true professional will further seek training and credentialing for the provision of mediation. Providing disputants with skilled, objective service helps them to find clarity and peace.

Objectivity, Neutrality & Non-Biased Practice

The skills of objectivity, neutrality, and non-biased practice are even more applicable to a pastoral mediator, because he may know both of the disputants. One disputant may have been a church member since childhood and the other for 15 years (since their marriage). The pastoral mediator may have also taught the disputants' mother, children or cousins in Sunday school class.

Therefore, the possibility for biased interpretations of a conflict can double and even triple if the disputants know (and are friends with) the pastor's family. It is *vital* to note that if the pastor is personally connected with the disputants, then he may first consider referring the disputants to another mediator or pastoral mediator before agreeing to mediate.

Referring Disputants that You Know

Referral is the appropriate procedure if the pastor is very close to the disputants. However, in some small town situations, pastors may consider serving as a pastoral mediator of church members that approach him for mediation if disputants have little or no alternative. Consider though, that their investment of time to drive to the next town may be best for them. Counselors have long since adapted to these situations by utilizing extra caution in their personal interactions. Counselors often refer individuals to other practitioners.

If the connection between the pastoral mediator and disputants can be kept *out* of personal interactions, then proceed with care and maintenance of objectivity and confidentiality. Remember that the guidelines, which govern privileged information, apply as well.

Privileged information includes all information shared in mediation. The distinction of privileged means that the mediator must not share his knowledge of any facts, discussion, or other information revealed in mediation with any other person or entity without the express permission (in writing) of all those participating in mediation. For additional information on privileged information, research your state's statutes regarding privileged information in mediation.

The Techniques of Mediation

The Mediator must know and have practiced the skills of mediation technique to the extent of being able to provide them with ease. These skills include:

- story-telling,
- caucusing,
- ground rules,
- brainstorming, using the flip chart/dry-erase board,
- compartmentalizing issues,
- resolution skills, and
- agreement writing skills

Practicing these techniques to mastery will free the mediator to provide the guidance that will be expected.

Storytelling

The mediator's talent in providing guidance comes through his or her ability to patiently listen to each disputant's side of the story. The technique of **storytelling** means allowing each disputant to tell his side of the story *without interruption from the other disputant.* The mediator listens with caring and gentle positive reinforcement. Questions to check for accuracy of facts may be then asked by the mediator first and the other side second. These questions are just to clarify points. The other "side" is then afforded the same respect when telling their side of the story and questions are allowed in the same manner.

The mediator is able to set the tone of the mediation process from the beginning of the discussion. He or she may make all the difference to the disputants, in that he/she may likely provide them with their first experience of talking about the dispute in this manner (no interruptions or judgments). This can change the tone of the entire conflict. When the mediator gives each side the equal respect and power of their position being equally valid and meaningful, perspectives of the disputants begin to change (even though they do not show this).

Caucusing

To take breaks during times of stress can change the conflict status. Taking a moment to breathe before saying something one might regret is important. Take a break during a moment that is most conducive to keeping the process flowing, but also "saves face," for both disputants. *(See "saving face" chapter four).*

During a **caucus,** the mediator meets with each "side" of a dispute alone. Sometimes, the disputants do not meet with the mediator, but rather, just take a break to meet together or talk with someone else about a fact or information. Then they return to the mediation to resume discussion.

If the mediator meets 15 minutes with one "side" he should also meet 15 minutes (no more no less) with the other side – keep it equal. This keeps the power balanced. Sometimes, mediators will meet 20 minutes with one side and only need to meet 5 minutes with the other. The mediator would then attempt to talk about something else with the (5-minute) side to fill up that extra 15 minutes of time. This preserves the equality of time spent with both sides and the perception of influence that the other respective side has of the private time spent with the mediator. During this caucus, it is also productive to the mediation to keep the focus of each conversation positive and centered on the objective at hand in mediation.

Ground Rules

Ground rules are usually established near the beginning of any conflict resolution process. One ground rule is that all who participate in such an activity to work genuinely toward a resolution.

Other common ground rules that disputants set include refraining from using curse words, *avoiding* negative initial judgments of new ideas or discounting any initial idea formed in brainstorming, and allowing each person the respect of finishing their statements without interruption.

Establishing these ground rules is important. They set a new tone for the discussion of a dispute based on mutual respect and equality. They further provide an expected guideline for behavior that likely has not been present in the disputants' interactions before. These guidelines permeate their work to seek options, ideas, and points of agreement. With ground rules, they may now view each other in a different manner as the mediation process continues. Disputants come up with their own ground rules; the practitioner does not simply write down ground rules.

It is much more powerful for the individuals (who will be solving the conflict) to write their own "rules" that govern how they will feel most respected and empowered. If the mediator simply gives the disputants ground rules, it is not as effective. The establishment of ground rules becomes the disputants' first successful agreement, and can set the stage for collaboration.

Brainstorming

The brainstorming process begins the new set of interactions between the disputants based on the ground rules that the disputants establish. **Brainstorming** is the solicitation of ideas (without judgment) from everyone in a room – with the goal of solving a problem. All ideas are accepted without judgment.The practitioner leading a brainstorm activity will usually say something to the effect of, "Give me your thoughts, ideas, options... for how this could be resolved."
The first objective for the brainstorming process is to agree on the set of problems that the mediation will work on. Every dispute contains a number of issues that can be worked through. It is the responsibility of the mediator to ask the disputants to prioritize which problems the mediation will address (more on this in the compartmentalizing section).

The brainstorming activity can take as long as necessary to solicit ideas. Often, mediators will go through several pages/stages of flip chart notes or dry-erase board re-writes, as the brainstormed ideas are written. It is best to use tear off pages from a flip chart for this process (or have a note-keeper or "recorder" take notes of the stages from a dry-erase board).

Recording Brainstormed Ideas

Professional facilitation uses a recorder, but it is fine for the mediator or a disputant to simply record brainstormed ideas for mediation. Both disputants should take turns recording if both are comfortable with this, to keep the perception of power balanced. The recorder could have a perceived greater amount of power if they recorded everything. When a mild power imbalance is present between disputants, this could be an effective way to balance a weaker disputant's power (who does not speak well) in the mediation.
The original ideas brainstormed are often refined as the work continues. It is a valuable exercise to go back and review pages written to access the ideas, options, and points established throughout the brainstorming process. Often, tiny points of agreement are stated then passed over.

These points need to be highlighted by the mediator before they are lost. Also, points of *challenge* need to be revisited. It is best if this is done using the exact words of the disputant.

As the brainstormed ideas take shape into an agreement, the notes from these pages can be referenced again. When the disputants begin to formulate options for an agreement, they may draw set of options to the problems from the pages of brainstormed work.

The Use of a Flip Chart/Dry-Erase Board

When using the **flip chart/dry-erase board**, I like to remember what my first academic mediation instructor taught me in doctoral school. Always bring a flip chart (or have access to a dry-erase board and markers). Make sure you write *something* on it – no matter what the *something* is.

This statement brought a smile to our faces as mediators, but the truth and validity of this good advice remains. Of course, as trained practitioners, we must use the skill and knowledge we have about resolving conflicts to write down what is important. However, the simple act of writing a small idea on a chart can serve to stimulate a new paradigm (*way of thinking and pathway toward a new option*) for the disputant.

Never discount the importance of simply writing something down on a different surface in front of the disputants. It stimulates Here are some options for what you could write. First, draw a line (dotted is best) vertically down the board/chart to represent an equal division of space and equal boundary between the two disputants. Use their *exact words* when writing down ideas, options, or questions to keep everyone on the same page.

TABLE 5   **Using A Flip Chart to Organize Ideas**

John's Ideas	Jane's Ideas
✓ child support paid monthly	✓ monthly child support payments
✓ payment date doesn't matter	✓ payment made by 5th

Item/Options to Write (for brainstorming):

- Dates & Times that Important Events Occurred
- Points of Agreement – as specific as possible
- Small facts, monetary amounts, individuals/places that disputants begin to show agreement on – assure that the writing of these facts will assist in resolution, rather than serve to further divide disputants

- Locations that are important to dispute
- Questions both or one side asks to facilitate a resolution
- Items that need to be "tabled" or discussed later
- Brainstormed Ideas/Options for solutions

You may separate any of these options into a separate page or heading to assist disputants to organize their facts or ideas. Feel free to re-write pages – but keep original drafts, as they may contain valuable bits of information about how concepts were reached.

Item/Options to Write (for agreement drafts):

- Begin with any small, specific point of agreement
- Compose small points into very simple statements
- Build on small simple points of agreement slowly, developing the foundation for more complex sentences that make up the next set of statements that both sides agree on

- The first draft of the agreement itself may be generated on the flip chart and later carried to the document draft.

Compartmentalizing Issues

As the disputants begin the resolution process, the mediator can provide his best assistance to these individuals by **compartmentalizing issues** or assisting disputants to break down their problems into solvable parts.

The problem(s) feel "overwhelming" to the disputants. When a professional guides them to look at the issues (*embedded within the problem(s)* one at a time, the disputants begin to feel empowered to both understand the problem(s) and find new options for resolution. This method of compartmentalizing issues helps disputants to feel that they can resolve small portions of their dispute.

Later, as they begin to solve small parts of their disagreement, their energy increases positively - to solve additional aspects of their problem. What once seemed unsolvable takes on a different perspective. That is the power of **mediation;** the ability of a third party professional to assist those in conflict toward a new set of perspectives that empower the individuals involved toward a more "reconciled" state of being. By breaking the problem down into solvable parts, the disputants further begin to identify options for an agreement.

Resolution Skill

The resolution skills needed to assist the disputants in discovering a set of solutions– comes from a mediator who has practiced his craft. **Resolution skill** is the mediator's ability to assist the disputants to see what points they *agree on* and *highlight these points* to the disputants. Points of agreement reveal much to them about *why* they agree and what *criteria* they use to agree.

Exploring why they agree and the criteria that they use to agree will allow them to compare and contrast the reasons that they disagree now. This level of analysis removes them from adversarial exchanges to a level *above* their dispute. To rise above their disagreement and seek understanding lays a foundation for resolution.

The new foundation they create in mediation for *recognizing* when they do agree and *building* on the strengths they discover will create a new pathway for them to find agreement for *this* dispute and for their disagreements in the future. Each component of the mediation process adds another layer of respect and equality on a situation that formerly was approached with anger, malice, loss, disappointment and sadness.

This opposite method of building a new foundation of clarity, respect, equality, empowerment, paced interactions, and recognition for small successes gained *transforms* the landscape of a dispute. These resolution skills serve to change the dispute into a workable entity that has a better chance of establishing an effective agreement.

Agreement Writing Skills

We have focused our attention in this chapter on the concrete skills needed to assist disputants through the structure of the mediation process. The final part of this process would be agreement-writing skills.

Agreement writing skills include the ability to condense points made by both disputants into a cohesive set of statements. As a mediator, your role at times becomes a bit schizophrenic. That is to say, you must do two opposite tasks simultaneously. You must be *open* to the exploration of new ways of approaching the dispute while at the same time listening for points of *agreement* that narrow down their general common interests.

Allowing the Disputants to Generate & Write the Agreement

Remember, it is the disputants who must generate and write the agreement. It is *their* agreement. It is their resolution and thereby must be their concept of what is just for them. Your thoughts about the specifics of an agreement (that you believe will work best for them) are best kept silent.

Allow the disputants to take credit for the tedious work of mediation, by allowing them the respect of writing what is best for them.

Trust that they will be able to come up with their own specifics. Allow them plenty of time to do so. Their agreement will be more powerful to them if they write it; the agreement will further have a better chance of be sustained by the disputants if they write it themselves. I include these directives because many mediators make the mistake of writing the agreement (using their own phrasing and statements). Many disputants ask the mediator to write the agreement.

Disputants *can* discover and write their own agreement. Their concept of the agreement will always be slightly different from even the most obvious options you can envision, If you sacrifice your own will to impose *your* concept of what is best to *their* better ability to write the agreement, they will be glad you did. In the long run, they can have a genuine feeling that they accomplished something difficult on their own.

Trust that Asking Questions is Enough

Mediators can ask questions in the agreement writing process. Mediators can offer options for respectful characterizations when asked to do so. Often, mediators create *leading* questions that may stimulate a resolution and the writing of a good sentence. Be careful in doing this and avoid it if possible. Trust that if you simply ask them to solve the specific points they have generated, that they can do this.

Your belief in the disputants' ability to write their own agreement will be their first and arguably most important professional reinforcement for doing so. Their own motivators of family obligations, financial obligations, and personal self-esteem will be just as important, but your faith in them to write their own agreement *on* their own will be a powerful positive reinforcement for them to do just that. Saying to them, "Remember how hard you worked on this point you established; I know your statement of this agreement will reflect that work," may *be* just the encouragement they need to place the more refined points into writing.

Specific Agreement Writing Skills:

1. The ability to listen and **write down** non-combative statements of agreement in simple, specific sentences.

2. The ability to assist disputants to refine and **edit** these simple sentences (keeping them as simple sentences) into statements that address each of their goals brought to mediation.

3. The ability to **ask general questions** that stimulate the ability of the disputants to continue to work on the completion of the agreement.

4. The **patience** to keep a steady slow pace and assure disputants that the work that they are doing to place into writing a respectful agreement will serve them well.

5. The ability to **keep the writing process going** when disputants become discouraged and frustrated. Going on to the next point and coming back to a challenging point instead of stopping the process is frequently needed.

6. The ability **to phrase** contentious points **in a respectful manner** that promotes collaboration and an equal reflection of both sides' perspective on each point.

7. The ability to **maintain a balance of power** throughout the writing of the agreement, to give equal attention to both sides' requests and stated needs.

8. The ability to **be flexible** to the need to return to the mediation process to explore points again with good listening skills and mediation techniques, if issues agreed upon turn to disagreement.

> Assure to first reinforce the motivations that points of agreement were based on in mediation. *Often, disputants second-guess themselves in the agreement writing process. A good mediator may be able to remind the disputants of the positive benefits established in mediation. Such a reminder may help solidify the foundation for agreement that was just established in the mediation.*

9. The ability to **thoroughly check** and double check the agreement for omissions, errors, grammatical presentation and spelling, as this document may be referred to repeatedly in the future, should the disputants return to *either* mediation or court.

10. The **knowledge of general forms** and procedures in state statutes (or the ability to access these) to reference any point of agreement that may be a cause for concern in the future.

Seeking Advisement from An Attorney

Many mediators may choose to refer disputant(s) to seek advisement from their attorney on points agreed on (for example: child support amounts) to assure that they are placing into writing a statement that can be maintained and will sustain over time. Caution, avoid referrals to adversarial attorneys. Adversarial attorney involvement (as opposed to a collaborative effort) can lead to a re-opening of the conflict.

Closing the mediation is the final part of the mediation process. Good closure in mediation is important that I have devoted a section of the final chapter of this book to the skills needed for closure. The caring, empathetic listening, and responding that goes into the closure process, permeates the entire process.

Chapter 9

Now write down for yourselves this song and teach it … and have them sing it so that they may be a witness...

- Deuteronomy 31:19

The *Guided* Method for Mediation Practice

The Guided Method of mediation is the technique that I personally use. It is an original theory of mediation practice. I have compiled several techniques that are popularly used in the practice of mediation. When applicable, I have noted the prior works that inspired me to create the steps in cited references. A condensed version of this method is included in this chapter. A subsequent text that expands upon this method is scheduled for publication as a follow up to this work.

Choices of Mediation Method

There are many methods of mediation. Some of the most prominent methods of mediation are referenced in this book. I believe any mediator would share with you that he uses a personal method of mediation that best suits his personality. You will do the same.

I feel it is important to note that an adherence to some standard methods of mediation practice is needed to insure and preserve the mediation process. This method includes techniques that I have found (as a doctorate level professional) are essential to the successful resolution of disputes.

Some professionals selecting this book as a resource may not have contemporary texts for mediation techniques – or may want a new perspective.

A Note About Forms Referenced

A **Contract for Mediation** Services is given to disputants to read and sign before entering into mediation. This contract usually includes an explanation of the mediation process and a statement of confidentiality. The contract is often mailed to participants prior to the first scheduled meeting date for their review and signatures.

A **Mediated Agreement** is a document generated by a mediator that specifies the points that both disputants agree to that resolve the dispute they had over a specific dispute. The resolution of the dispute is often placed on a form called a **Memorandum of Understanding**, which specifies the points of agreement between the two parties. The mediated agreement (or *memorandum of understanding* – depending on forms standard by state) is signed and dated by disputants, the mediator, and often a witness. The agreement may further be presented to a notary republic (subject to state procedure) to further validate the points agreed on.

Points of Agreement can address each issue that was disputed by the individuals seeking mediation. Mediated agreements clearly detail how each point will be resolved specifically, stating the actions required of both disputants. Sometimes, mediated agreements assist disputing parties to simplify more complex legal suits, such as divorce cases. Often, however, individuals in conflict may utilize the professional practice of mediation to resolve their dispute in lieu of more extensive litigation.

The **Confidentiality Statement** clearly defines that the mediation is confidential and that all disputants who participate in mediating a dispute agree to maintain the confidentiality of all information shared in the mediation. The limits to confidentiality are clearly outlined.

All participants must sign the confidentiality statement. Signing indicates their agreement to maintain confidentiality. There are limits to confidentiality. These are outlined in the confidentiality form and follow state guidelines for the report of abuse and stated intent to harm. Examples of typical mediation forms such as the confidentiality statement, contract for mediation, and memorandum for understanding can be found in Appendix A of this work.

The *Guided* **Method** for Mediation Practice
Condensed Version

The *Environment*

1. **Arrange the disputants around a circular or oblong table**. Avoid rectangular or square tables which literally "square" off individuals against one another. If you must use a rectangular table, then gather individuals around one end to form an approximated circle.

2. **Assure that you have both a legal pad and dry marker board or flip chart with you**. You should have several colored markers, eraser, liquid dry marker board cleaner, and more than one color of pen. Assure the room you use has a temperature pleasing to all persons in the room. Check the décor for aesthetic presentation. Assure that rest rooms are close by and that a drink and/or snack machine is available. Providing healthy snacks to disputants is acceptable and promotes an atmosphere of care and acknowledgement of the equal need of survival (hunger) that all humans have alike.

3. **Assure chairs are comfortable** and that all individuals participating have access to pencil, paper, and a calendar should be present (you bring or one should be in the room for reference).

4. **Bring a calculator and any other materials**, books, reports, that may be relevant to the mediation at hand.

Your *Preparations*

5. **Make a thorough study of the conflict, noting all motivators** and possible variables hat may influence each set of sides toward either a resolution or deeper dispute.

6. **Make yourself brief notes** of the possible motivators that each side has for resolving the dispute. Do not show these to the disputants.

7. **Be prepared and ready to write on the dry marker board at any time** throughout the mediation to emphasize points – especially points both agree on.

8. **Write down ANY point** (however minuscule) **that both sides agree on.** Assure to adhere to the ground rules that have been established above for avoiding curse words and derogatory characterizations.

1. **The mediator then is allowed to ask the first side questions to clarify his story and position.** The mediation then asks: "What do you want to happen?" and allows for response.

2. **The opposing side may then ask questions** to clarify the *story* only (but not simultaneously with the mediator). This prevents either side from feeling attacked with questions by both.

3. **The opposing disputant then gets the same respect of telling his story without interruption** and the pattern of asking questions repeats equally. The mediator would ask the same final question of the opposing disputant when he finishes his story: "What do you want to happen?" and allows for response.

4. **The mediator then may ask both sides questions. Then both sides may ask questions** – to clarify the story facts only. Again, the disputants wait a respectful amount of time before firing responses. The mediator will interrupt and remind disputants of ground rules if needed or simply interrupt and a comment or clarifying question to assure that the discussions are proceeding with respect.

5. **The mediator closes story-telling by summarizing all points made by each side after each has finished speaking** to keep the group focused on the objective of reaching   a resolution. He further summarizes both stories before continuing the mediation to check for clarity and accuracy of points.

6. **The mediator gives a brief, non-judgmental reflective summary of the points and continued objectives.** Use the following statement at the end of each summary: "What I heard you say that you agree on is…"

Continuing the Mediation

7. **Write down ideas for resolution/clarification** on the flip chart or dry marker board in a   brainstorming   activity.   **Record   all   brainstormed ideas**. This helps re-focus the group on resolution and gives another opportunity for summarization.

8. **The mediator continues generating options** with both sides, working to maintain an equal representation of ideas from both sides. The mediator should work to maintain an equal power balance (defined either by *number of people in room, speaking time, and force of personality*) between disputants.

Answers from the "weaker" side *(if there is one)* **may be written on the dry marker board first and the   stronger side second** but with equal weight. All answers are accepted. (*do not write curse words on the board or negative comments*). This method of asking the weaker side *first* helps to balance the power between the two sides, which promotes a more equitable discussion.

9. **As a mediator, you should always seize two types of opportunities** within the mediation.

> 1 – To strongly emphasize points the two sides **agree on**
>   (no matter how small) and
> 2 – To **balance the power** between the two opposing sides at
>   every opportunity possible by giving speaking time to a
>   weaker   side if the "stronger" side is monopolizing time
>   in the mediation

10. **Answers from both sides are formulated and written into goals on the dry marker board first and revised on paper as the work continues.** All options for goals are accepted initially and refined into workable goals that focus the mediation on the objectives for the mediated agreement

11. **The mediator then works with both sides to translate the goals of mediation into one to two well-defined problems that the disputants have been facing.** These statements of their problems will help the mediator to define criteria for the resolution that they will draft an agreement to address

12. **Create a short list of criteria for resolution to these goals & problems.**
    The list may look similar to this:

Criteria for Success	Goal

Visitations are equal for holidays
    Children share Holiday visitation
    time w/both parents
	Agreement on holidays

You may write an example criterion –to help them understand. Write a simple criterion for each goal and problem. Generating a list of criteria may be a challenge for disputants, but work patiently with them if they have difficulty in writing criteria that they *both* agree on. Assure that both disputants agree to all criteria, to prevent problems later for them in both *implementing* and *sustaining* an agreement they have written.

13. Use the "Parking Lot" Technique to help disputants who are "stuck" and are unable to conceptualize alternatives (this can be used in the step above as well). It helps disputants who are having a hard time coming up with options - to "park" ideas – similar to filling in cars in a parking lot.

_____	_____
_____	_Visit alternate days of week___
_____	_____
_____	_____

Flip your chart or erase your dry marker board & start with a clean front. **Draw blanks** and tell disputants that this is a parking lot for ideas and possibly take the first step of **supplying an example idea.**

14. **Now write down ideas for solutions in the blanks** from anyone in the room – be sure to emphasize point both sides agree on.

15. On a separate page – Write a heading – "**Agree On**" and begin listing any and all points they agree on –no matter how minuscule.

<u>Agree On</u>

_____

_____

_____

16. As an agreement begins to take form – you as mediator should **sit down at certain points and write down full sentences of agreement on your legal pad.**

Finalizing a *Resolution*

17. **When an agreement begins to take shape, stay seated and work with both sides**, emphasizing a balance of power and write down the agreement they begin to create. Use their words.

18. **Do not suggest solutions**. If disputants ask you for a solution, ask them what they think would work best for them.

19. **Continue to emphasize their ability to resolve this** because they know more than anyone about the dispute and what would best resolve it for them.

Writing the *Agreement*

1. **Take as much time as needed** to write down a resolution that addresses all issues brought forth by the disputants as important to them for a satisfactory outcome. Smaller issues may be tabled for later, unless they directly pertain to the issues of highest priority.

2. **Have the disputants prioritize the most important issues** (as the mediator, resist prioritizing for   them – ask them what is important)

3. **Write down a final resolution, which includes all points**. Do not hesitate to re-write the resolution.

4. **Expect the writing to take a long time**. Tell disputants to expect this as well so they will not be frustrated. Let them know that this is a good sign that they are putting together an agreement that will better address their dispute.

Chapter 10

Closing Mediation with Care & Thoroughness

Closure is a vital component of any cathartic event in one's life. This belief stems from the theories of Gestalt therapy, popularized in the late 1950's (Perls, 1973). Closure in this context, denoted a "process of completing the [formerly] incomplete circle," (Luchins & Luchins, 1999, p.1).

Closure

Closure

What is closure? I describe **closure** for my students of conflict resolution as having a sense of psychological certainty or completeness when a life event ends. The writing of a good resolution to a conflict is *one* type of life event.

Closure is a vital component of any cathartic event in one's life. This belief stems from the theories of Gestalt therapy, popularized in the late 1950's by Fritz Perls (1973). Closure in this context, denoted a "process of completing the [formerly] incomplete circle," (Luchins & Luchins, 1999, p.1). The Gestalt theory presented the concept of closure as a necessary component of the resolution of conflict. Indeed, this theory stated that outcome measures of conflicts *that had not reported an adequate reach of "closure"* were less successful than those who did report a "closure," of open issues.

These descriptions of closure and their importance in resolving issues reveals that this final process of resolution is just as important as the beginning and middle of the mediation process. To open a festering wound without properly completing treatment of the infection within, leaves the laceration exposed and vulnerable to even deeper hurt. Just as any wound leaves the area it affects more open to greater harm, so does the opening of a dispute have the potential to more deeply harm those it affects without proper closure.

Recognizing When a Dispute is Nearing Closure

To recognize when a dispute is nearing closure is a skill required of a professional mediator. The variables that signal closure are invisible to disputants. Even if they recognize these signs, they are often tempted to re-instigate other aspects of the conflict. A dispute is nearing closure when

- disputants begin to reach agreement on most of the points they have brought into the mediation process, and
- disputants begin to signal that they are at a better position emotionally.

TABLE 6   Physical Signs of Closure

Some physical signs of closure to watch for include:

✓ Both disputants nodding their head in agreement to a number of concepts, while simultaneously exhibiting

✓ Several exhales of breath (*from both disputants*) over an hour of time (indicating a steady release of tension)

✓ Body positions turn from a *closed* stance to an *open* stance
(*indicating that disputants are more open to the other sides' perspective*)

✓ Facial expressions appear relieved and more complacent

I have observed this small collection of observations over years of time in mediating cases. Paul Elmore (2008) notes a long list of behaviors that many counselors observe that are similar to the signs listed above. Below I have re-written his list to include clear signs of when a client is showing closure.

TABLE 7   12 Closure Signals

> ### Signals to Recognize when a Client is Showing Closure
>
> 1. Has confidence in one's identity
> 2. Feels able to express and receive both positive & negative emotions in a respectful manner
> 3. Identifies strengths and weaknesses
> 4. Self-talk is appropriate and realistic
> 5. Able to discuss their story openly and completely
> 6. Can ask and seek help
> 7. Able to handle small disagreements
> 8. Able to grant forgiveness to self & others
> 9. Feels good about using their voice
> 10. Uses personal power appropriately
> 11. Less anxiety and/or anxiety feels manageable
> 12. Client Goals Met

These non-verbal indicators along with other verbal statements indicate that the disputants have reached a new position in their beliefs about their problems. Disputants often make statements such as, "I think that is true also (agreeing with the other side)." Or "I believe we have accomplished a lot with these meetings."

When disputants begin to tell you this, believe them. Even if they have not reached agreement on every point, they are indicating that they feel a sense of accomplishment on the points that have been successfully talking through. Giving both recognition and validity to this sense of accomplishment is an important component for disputants to realize. A sense of accomplishment (in finding points of agreement) enables disputants to lay a foundation for a good resolution.

Taking Time to Consider the Agreement

If the disputants take the rest of that day (following the writing of the first draft) to rest from mediation and get a good night's sleep then this is conducive to the writing of a good agreement. They will be fresher on their return and have the energy necessary to focus on the details of the agreement. The time they take to consider their points of agreement gives them the ability to talk about the specifics with family. Allowing them time to talk with family may assure that they have not left out important considerations that can be adjusted during the writing process. It is best to *not* allow *too much* time to pass between the work to draft an agreement in mediation and the writing of the final agreement.

If the writing of the final agreement can begin the next day or within one day, this is best. Too much time will allow doubt to creep into the minds of the disputants and may undo some of the hard work toward resolution. The writing of the agreement is the disputants' final opportunity to work through this dispute in mediation. In my experience as a mediator, some of the best work in the mediation process takes place during the writing of the agreement. For it is in the writing of the specific points that the disputants agree to, that you as the mediator see them at their best.

When disputants see these new responsibilities in writing, their agreement becomes tangible, and they begin to consider consequences, fairness, and equability. The work that they have done to forge an agreement turns from an "ideal" to something **real** and this change in perspective, often causes changes in the agreement.

Changes in the Agreement

It is important to not react with shock if the agreement (so tediously worked on in the mediation) suddenly changes. Trust that the mediation process is working. The agreement that begins to take shape in this final section of the process represents the disputants' evolution of their problem. Do not allow them to throw out points they have agreed on, just refine them.

Continue to assure that you as the mediator are not influencing the outcome of the agreement by suggesting solutions or adaptations. Allow the disputants to drive the writing of their own dispute, and they will get closer and closer (as they adapt the writing) to an agreement that will work for them. Sometimes, agreements have to be amended in the future, but remember that future agreements would not have been possible if the work to reach an original agreement had not been accomplished. If you trust the process, the disputants will likely place into writing an agreement that will be more sustainable.

Sustainable Agreements

Sustainable agreements often are refined a number of times. Sometimes, points are changed entirely. This can be fine if both disputants wholeheartedly agree to *new* points of agreement and the replacement of other points. Mediators who are just starting out will need to be aware that the process of closure and writing of the agreement takes even more patience than the beginning and middle of the mediation. The more you as the mediator are able to role-model patience, the more you will be able to stimulate the disputants to work steadily toward the writing of an agreement that will work for them over time.

Final "Airing"

Both parties' feelings about the agreement must be aired and validated separately (*accepted as true and worthy of consideration*). Without this validation, consideration and respect, the agreement will not be sustained. Both sides must feel equally that they have been respected and the necessary components of *their* dispute have been addressed. When both parties feel that their position has been validated and that they have reached the best agreement that they can come to with the other disputant, they will let you know both verbally and non-verbally.

Remember, the disputants' priorities ARE the priorities. Your priorities as the mediator (in terms of *your perception* of what they should prioritize) are not. Disputants' priorities are more valid to their conflict. They are the only ones who know why, and they are not always able to tell you why. If they feel that they have reached closure on an issue or set of issues, they are right. It is your job to re-prioritize your perception of their conflict as they see fit and write up the agreements that they have reached. Never let your own priorities for closure and agreement guide the mediation.

TABLE 8   A Mediator's Dilemma

To Agree or Not Agree

A set of disputants begin to agree on payments one will make to another. You see the signs of agreement. You may feel that the amount they have agreed on is not correct, but you accept the agreement that they have made.

As you begin to write up the agreement, one side begins to talk about how much salary she makes. Her statement about salary does not directly relate to their agreement about payments made, but you have a dilemma. Her salary and the payments being discussed seem out of line. Do you continue to write the agreement they have made about payments?

Let the Disputants' Decide

This is an oft-faced problem for a mediator. Wait. Allow the disputants to figure this out alone without imposing your influence. Simply stop writing. If they ask your opinion, redirect them by saying, "You both have discovered something to consider. What do each of you think is equitable?" They will be able to decide on an amount they agree, or they will discuss the matter further if they do not agree. These small dilemmas are common in the agreement-writing phase. Take the time you need to take to resolve the refinement issues. You can do this in the agreement writing phase and return back to the mediation by using phrases that will lead the disputants like, "I am glad that we took the time to refine this; to do so will insure a more sustainable agreement."

Prepare Disputants: This Will Take Time

To tell disputants that, "we are nearly done," does *not* do them a service. Disputants will be annoyed as the agreement is refined and may agree to changes because they feel that "we should have been done by now." Best to prepare them up front that "you have saved the best for last, and it takes the most successful clients several hours to complete this well." Clients who do take their time are much happier with the results.

Final Phase of Mediation

When the agreement has been written, one of the best options to select is taking a break. The break should last at least 20 minutes and it is better if both disputants have the opportunity to both eat and drink. The best-case scenario is for the disputants to take a lunch or dinner break, come back the next day, and begin the final process. As discussed earlier, a long break that includes dinner, lunch and preferably a night's sleep allows disputants to refresh themselves and absorb the change in the work they have done.

You will not be able to fully reach closure and accept the agreement they have placed into writing if you are not able to stimulate them to accept this change in the work of mediation without you present. Disputants must consider the consequences of the agreement outside of your influence to be able to envision how it will be realized in their world. This will serve to help solidify the validity of the work they have done.

Initiating Closure

If disputants resist their own instincts to reach closure, it may indicate that they have other unresolved issues. Often, these issues are individualistic and apply only peripherally to the dispute in question. In other words, their own internal conflicts may be holding them back from resolving the dispute – even though the work they have done to resolve it constitutes resolution. Only disputants can truly decide whether they have reached closure, and it is best to allow them to initiate closure.

In many cases, disputants do not give clear signals and it is beneficial for the mediator to "test the waters" and assess whether or not the signs he is seeing of closure (on the issues brought for *mediation*) are resolved. In these instances, the mediator must initiate closure and assess the disputants' reactions. Ask of both sides: "How do you feel about this agreement?"

Follow-Up

Following up after mediation is very important to all parties involved. The mediator will benefit from follow-ups to former clients, as he will be silently thanked for the caring call and may again be of assistance to those he follows up with.

Disputants will indeed appreciate the follow up call that you place to check on how they are doing. They will immediately recognize the care you take to remember specifics of their dispute that they succeeded on. They will appreciate that you are kind enough to remember how much the hard work they did meant to their resolution.

Take time to follow-up. You may also uncover the need for additional mediation or other needs for counseling or legal help. Have a list of referral sources at your ready disposal so that you can refer former clients to someone else to help them that you know and trust. Also, assure that you have checked your own availability to provide a follow up mediation to the disputants if they request this.

It is uncommon for disputants to return to mediation over the very same issues, but it does happen. What happens more often is that disputants return to mediate another issue. They often refer someone else to mediation, because they have had a good experience with you and appreciate that you cared enough to call them to follow up.

Chapter 11

Obey your leaders and submit to their authority. They keep watch over you as men who must give an account. Obey them so that their work will be a joy, not a burden...

- Hebrews 13:17

Mediator Credentials: The Need for Credibility

When pastors, bishops, vicars and other church ministers have met with individuals in crisis in the past, these meetings have been informal and often described as counseling. Few ministers are actually credentialed to mediate, so the resolution of conflicts by pastors has not followed an established structure.

Obtaining Credentials

It is advisable for the pastoral mediator to establish his credentials in the state he plans to practice in. Within many state court systems, the state bar or State Supreme Court oversees the practice of mediation. Many states also specify guidelines for outside professionals (non-attorneys) for obtaining credentials to mediate. To become credentialed, one has only to read these guidelines and begin the process that is specified for your state. Some states do not have a codified process for obtaining mediation credentials, but many states are in the process of determining guidelines for mediation credentials.

Obtaining mediation credentials is usually a bit costly and can take as long as a year or more to complete, but to a pastor who is seriously interested in providing pastoral mediation services, becoming certified, registered, or credentialed through your state's court system is best.

Disputes often end up in court, and every dispute carries with it the threat of court intervention. Therefore, to establish your credentials through your state's process for credentialing mediators creates accountability for you and validity of your ability to provide mediation. You want to provide a service that is recognized within *your* state's court process.

Upon the writing of this work, the national Association for Conflict Resolution (ACR) is in the process of developing national guidelines for mediation credentials. This author is one of several professionals that have worked with the ACR to research and establish a consistent set of national credentials for mediators. The work to establish *consistent* credentials has been tedious and slow to manifest. These credentialing guidelines are not in place throughout the United States in 2014. Credentialing standards, protocols, training requirements and titling differs still by state. A list of credentialing references for each state is provided in Appendix B.

Differences between States

Each state has a separate set of norms and guidelines that govern the practice of mediation. Each state further specifies how mediation agreements or "Memorandums of Understanding" must be written, filed, and processed through that state's court system. Not all states use Memorandums of Understanding.

Each state processes divorces within its "domestic" court (categorized differently by state) Non-divorce cases are categorized into the superior, criminal or general court level that applies to each state respectively.

State Variations & Similarities

States vary as widely in their requirements for professional mediator qualification as they do in geographic placement within the nation. Many states do have an entity within their state court system that oversees the provision of mediation; however, a number of states are in the process of developing a set of protocols for the provision of "court mediation."

Court mediation refers to any specific mediation that either is *generated* in court or may see its ultimate resolution in a court of law. It is important to note that any dispute may be brought to a court of law at some point so to treat all disputes as if they may be "heard" in court is a prudent practice.

Certification, Registry, & Directories
Certification

Some states that **certify** mediators have enacted statutory legislation regarding mediation provision. A few states mandate that professionals become certified in order to perform mediation services in selected divisions of their respective courts. Generalizations to define certification practice between most states are nearly impossible to make, as each of the fifty states and the District of Columbia differs slightly in the guidelines present for court mediation.

Table seven notes that some states certify mediators in a manner that "varies by type." This means that different levels of their court system (superior, district ...) have different requirements and types of mediation for the disputes that exist in that type or level of court.

Many states require certification of mediators through an approved training program, as defined by their state court's guidelines for mediation training and certification. There are also other requirements (*besides training*) for mediators to become certified. These requirements include hours of observation and mentoring by certified mediators.

State training programs that certify mediators are private organizations who have met the requirements for state certification training. This simply means that training programs for mediation *often* must meet state guidelines in order for their training to be accepted toward certification or registry. Many states are "moving toward" certification. This means that their requirements for credentialing mediators contain many of the same objectives for certification, used by other states.

51 Sets of Qualifications, 51 Differences

It is important to note here that upon the writing and research of this work, each of the fifty states and the District of Columbia varies so completely (with regard to mediator qualification) that a standard for exact comparison is nearly impossible still in 2014. This table of comparison is an attempt to document the research done by this author to compare the vast differences between states and to further the knowledge of how mediator qualifications differ (by state).

Errors in interpretation may exist; it is best to consult the websites listed for the most current developments of mediator qualifications. In many states, mediator qualifications vary by county and vary by region. These inconsistencies in mediator qualification create problems for both the public and professional mediator. I hope that court systems within each state will move toward consistency so that the public will understand mediation as both an alternative and supplement to litigation.

Registry

States that have established a registry of mediators require mediators to undergo training and other requirements in order to be **registered** by that state's court system. Mediators who are registered have been "approved" to provide mediation by members of that state's entity, which oversees mediator qualifications.

The qualifications for registry closely mirror the qualifications for certification. Private training programs (that have been approved by that state's court system) can provide mediator training for registry. Other requirements for registry also exist and again often mirror the requirements for *certification* set forth in many other states.

States that are "moving toward" registry appear (upon the research of this work) to exhibit many of the same guidelines outlined in other states that register mediators – which indicated to this author that the state was in a process of developing a registry or roster of approved professional mediators. Registered mediators carry much the same "weight" or professional validity (*as far as training and other court requirements*) as certified mediators.

Directories & No Requirements

States, which simply have a directory, vary even more vastly in establishment of mediator qualifications than do states with certification and registry requirements. Some of these states are very close to establishing either certification or registry standards. Many of these states appear to have few or no requirements for professional mediator qualifications.

If a mediator lives in such a state, he is encouraged to become credentialed on his own. Many states encourage voluntary certification and training in their court guidelines for alternative dispute resolution, but lack generalized requirements for state professional practice. Mediators who *voluntarily* seek credentialing in these states offer the public a much more enhanced mediation experience.

Mediator directories that are run by private for profit web agencies and training programs abound. Most states that do not have an established set of mediator qualifications *do* have an immediate link available to them for private mediation training. Mediators in these states frequently pay a fee to be listed on a directory of mediators. These "For Profit" programs do actually benefit areas of our country that do not have established protocols for the provision mediation service and training. Refer to the links provided for each state in Table 8 for more information.

Moving Toward Certification, Registry, & Consistency

It is further important to note that nearly *all* of the states within our country are in a process of on-going development of their mediation programs. Upon the date of this research, many state court systems seem stymied in their development of mediator qualification requirements.

Much of the information that I located on state court websites was between two and five years old. Some states' guidelines were older. It is time for states to update their research, but professionals must abide by the standards that exist.

Many new schools of dispute and conflict resolution have been created across the country in the last five years. However, the development of new mediation theory has slowed in this first decade of the 21st century. State court systems need continued prompting to include consistent guidelines for mediator training and service provision.

If you live in a state that is "moving toward" certification or registry, then do your own research. Discover how you can become a catalyst for improvement of mediation standard and consistency in your state.

To Begin the Credentialing Process

The mediator must begin his understanding of each state's mediator qualification process by first learning how to find the court guidelines that govern the practice of mediation in your state. The next steps involve familiarizing oneself with mediator qualifications and training standards required by that state. Sometimes, it can be beneficial to know the guidelines of a neighboring state as well.

Many members of the public may have once lived in the state that borders the one in which you intend to practice. Knowledge of bordering states' mediation guidelines becomes immediately relevant in these cases. However, the court statutes, norms, and provision model *for your state* matters first and foremost, since any and all disputes may *first* go through the court of the state the *disputants* currently reside in. Mediators should read thoroughly about how mediations are conducted in each state, including how the agreements are written, paid for, and processed through the court.

Steps in Credentialing

Next, you will need to locate a couple of training programs within your state and decide which of the programs you feel is best for you. Try not to make your decision based on the fee. Remember that your qualifications to mediate will determine the quality of the service you provide. You need the best training you are able to locate and attend. Most private programs provide either 20 or 40 hours of training. Assure that the program you select is accepted by the court system in your state.

It is important to know also that most programs require a new mediator to observe a number of mediations (sometimes more than one type) under the supervision of a state approved mentor. Check your state's guidelines, as each state differs *greatly* in these requirements, but most have a component of observation.

Becoming a Non-Attorney Mediator

Many states require that mediators are also attorneys. Some few states only allow attorneys to become credentialed to mediate within that state's court system. Most states however, accept outside professionals in their credentialing program, but they frequently have a separate set of guidelines for non-attorney mediators.

Even if you plan to practice mediation in a state that only credentials attorneys, it is still advisable to obtain your own mediation credentials. Most mediators list their training and observation credentials in their professional descriptions on private websites, pamphlets or professional listings.

To budget one's schedule and financial investments to *acquire* and *maintain* credentialing is a requirement of *any* professional seeking a long-term career. As the conflicts in our world continue to intensify and economic stressors mount, the need for good, caring mediation services is sure to remain constant.

Challenge of Mediating Without Credentials

If a pastoral mediator is not credentialed, he faces a number of challenges initially. Any profession that is new and not yet established in the eyes of the general public will undergo much scrutiny.

Thirty years or more after the initial creation of this field, the practice of mediation is still considered new and uncharted territory by many members of the public. Individuals in conflict feel awkward about this state of being, and often transfer their awkward feelings into extra scrutiny. It may not make "sense," but it is a reality that individuals who feel awkward, embarrassed, ashamed, and scared of their situation doubt any intrusion into this vulnerable state of being.

Lack of Credentials

Expect challenge. Actually, when one considers this obstacle, it is important to remember that pastors are often faced with a similar set of challenges. Ministers face doubting on-lookers each week, as they delve into the most vulnerable aspects of the lives of their congregate. Congregation members often pause and consider the inspirational questions posed and sometimes challenge the lessons revealed. To withstand challenges, the professional minister has his ministerial training to back up his knowledge of his profession.

If the pastoral mediator is not credentialed, the good work that can be accomplished is compromised when a disputant falls into denial and blames the pastoral mediator. To anticipate this will prevent the disputant from initiating this line of denial. The mediator's validity (established through the credentialing process) will more powerfully stimulate the disputant to believe what you have to say.

Assets of Pastoral Mediators: Bridging the Gap

Pastoral mediators who are credentialed can offer the field of mediation a wealth of professional knowledge and service. Pastoral mediators may even be able to bridge the gap between public suspicion and public willingness to accept mediation as a viable alternative to litigation.

The credibility of pastors to provide solace to those in need – in times of conflict and pain is well established in decades of selfless service. Transferring this credibility is possible when pastors obtain the skills needed to provide credentialed mediation.

The bridge between general public acceptance and integration into the greater mythos of dispute resolution services may lie within the reach of pastors because there is much credibility inherent in the provision of ministry to the masses.

As we enter the 21st century, to be able to provide members of congregates and the public a more holistic method of mediation provision serves to benefit all. With patience and understanding, the credentialing process is only a matter of time and dedication.

Part III

Secular Versus Pastoral Mediation

Chapter 12

But Jehoshaphat also said to the King of Israel. 'First seek the counsel of the Lord.

- I Kings 22:5

Types of Mediation that Can Be Brought To a Pastoral Mediator

Historically, the disputes brought to a pastor have been "domestic," in nature. In general, mediations that involve families, neighbors, friends, divorces, child custody, estate planning mediation, and sometimes, victim advocacy … lend themselves well to pastoral intervention.

Mediations that involve insurance claim settlement, business law negotiations, landlord tenant disputes, and other judicial process mediations are best addressed in secular mediation.

Divorce Mediation

Divorce mediation(s) have lent themselves well to intervention that is lead by a pastor. The promise of a more caring and less "stigmatized" intervention for a divorce has led couples to seek evangelical guidance for mediation.

How Pastoral Mediation Can Better Address Divorce Mediation

In divorce mediation, the resolution of marital property is better addressed through a holistic resolution that meets the needs of both husband and wife equally and respects the needs of the children as well.

Pastoral mediators are able to stimulate a more holistic resolution through the use of positively created goals. The initial focus in pastoral mediation of a spirit of "reconciliation," frames the dispute from the perspective that the two parties can come together to reach a resolution that benefits *all*. Pastoral mediation develops an atmosphere in which all individuals involved are *able* to grow positively from the experience.

Family Financial/Settlement

Many states divide divorce mediation into two categories. One type focuses on issues of property division and settlement, leaving the objectives of child custody and visitation to a separate division (*more in chapter two*).

The specifics of property division are best mediated with the assistance of the attorneys that advise both litigants. There are important legal statutes and guidelines that both disputants will need guidance with from their attorneys. It is important to the disputants to write an agreement on property issues that will be sustainable.

The negotiations between both sets of disputants and their attorneys respectively are often combative and fraught with threats of legal suit. To minimize the threat of intensive litigation, the disputants can seek a pastoral mediator to reach better agreements regarding the property they are now in need of dividing.

How Pastoral Mediation Can Better Address Property Division

A pastoral mediator will help them to "air" thoughts and feelings in a more safe and supportive environment. Having the ability to discuss contentious issues in a more supportive setting reduces the possibility of deeper controversy in higher paid legal time.

Whether aware of this or not, each disputant has emotional associations with the property they will now divide in a divorce. A Pastoral Mediator is able to work with disputants in an atmosphere of caring and trust. They can encourage disputants to work through their emotional attachments to the properties being divided, enabling them to use their time with attorneys more efficiently.

Child Custody or Family Evaluations

As discussed in chapter two, the division of divorce mediation between child custody and property settlement assists individuals in divorces to place the appropriate amount of focus on their children.

Child custody mediation lends itself well to pastoral intervention, as the patience and caring that is needed to focus divorcing parents on the best needs for their children is paramount. Pastors often possess the ability to better guide individuals toward a position of positive resolution, based on their ministerial training and background.

How Pastoral Mediation Can Better Address Child Custody

Couples in a divorce mediation often fight over the larger issues embedded in child visitation. Mediation focuses them on selecting which holidays and birthdays they will equally share each year. A holistic goal they could next work on is creating a schedule for visitation that will make the *child(ren)* the most happy. Considering the best needs of the children first (*before the needs of the parents*) is a positive goal for the problem of visitation that a pastoral mediator could address.

Disputants will bring up every aspect of this visitation problem. When they are gently guided (from the inception of the mediation) to remember the best needs of the children *first*, a more positive resolution will be promoted – removing the focus from the opposing goals of each disputant alone.

Domestic Disputes

Many other "domestic disputes" could be served by pastoral mediation. Divorce cases are the most popular domestic conflicts that come to pastoral mediation, but they are not the only types of mediation that can be brought to a pastoral mediator. Most domestic disputes (that often end up in the court system) could be brought to a pastoral mediator.

For instance, the in state of North Carolina there is a form of mediation entitled, "Pre-litigation Farm Nuisance Mediation," that is undertaken between farmers with members of industry or neighborhood homeowner organizations to settle possible property devaluation issues.

How Pastoral Mediation Can Better Address Domestic Disputes

Domestic disputes would be well suited to pastoral mediation. They involve the resolution of conflicts between individuals that are often personal. The resolution of these types of disputes requires an understanding of emotional issues.

A caring resolution from a positive focus can promote the long term healing and understanding that is needed for interpersonal disputes that are usually emotional. In most domestic disputes, the issues of contention are very specific, and therefore require very specialized forms of resolution.

Estate Planning

Estate planning mediation is a new specialization within the field of mediation that is well suited for pastoral mediation. Families seek estate-planning mediation to assist them in settling the issues surrounding the final division of property of a family member.

When a family member dies, there are both emotional *and* property issues needing resolution. The property settlement process often brings up family conflicts that need to be resolved first (before properties can be dispersed and tasks assigned for final document preparation). Estate planning mediation was created to provide a forum for families needing to resolve these issues.

In order for the dispersing of property and process of paperwork to even *begin*, these contentious issues (left over from unresolved family conflicts) often have to be resolved. Without estate planning mediation, many families waste precious legal time in dispute.

How Pastoral Mediation Can Better Address Estate Planning

The need for a mediator who provides a caring and reconciliatory approach is clear in estate planning mediation. If the family's pastor is not in a position to provide unbiased help, then he may refer the family to another pastoral mediator in the same denomination.

Pastors are seen as respected members of a family's community. Pastoral mediation provides a safe neutral haven for the opening of conflicts that have lived in a family for many years. Often, families have long associations with churches and this association can form a common bond between family members of different faiths.

For example, if siblings have been raised in one denomination, but as adults, join another, they may differ on denomination in life, but find common ground with using a pastoral mediator. The pastoral mediator is able to make both siblings feel safe because the family members trust the ability of a pastor to care about the resolution of their family's dispute.

Victim's Advocates

Victims' advocacy is a specialized profession grounded in police departments and community service organizations.

In mediation between the victim and the convicted offender, the victim confronts the offender about the crimes the offender committed (that pertain to this victim). The goal of the mediation is for the victim and offender to reach resolution over the emotional aspects of these crimes. Both seek to resolve the consequences of the crimes in question (see *epilogue* for additional reference).

How Pastoral Mediation Can Better Address Victim's Advocacy

Victims' advocacy mediation uses a *facilitative style* (see chapter seven) of mediation practice. The goal of victims' advocacy is to accomplish a transformative objective – to stimulate both victim and offender to heal. A pastoral mediator can utilize a more facilitative style of mediation because he is able to create an atmosphere that is positively focused and may better promote with his role as spiritual leader, a more transformative frame of reference.

Pastoral mediators may frame the interactions in the mediation (chapter six) in a manner that is designed to encourage a safe environment and empower disputants to share needed emotions. He is able to use the skills of mediation to maintain boundaries and focus interactions toward positive goals. These techniques, delivered by a pastoral mediator with a caring, positive focus, help disputants to stimulate healing.

Limits of Pastoral Mediation

The opportunity for pastoral mediation intervene in family, friend, and neighbor disputes does have limits. The frame of mind that "all conflicts that go to a secular mediator – can also be brought to a pastoral mediator" is not accurate. A mediator that is more trained and focused in judicial process best deals with some disputes.

Chapter 13

And I charged your judges at that time: Hear the disputes between your brothers and judge fairly...

- Deuteronomy 1:16

Types of Mediation Better Suited To Secular Practice

This chapter focuses on the types of dispute resolution practice that are best suited for professionals in the secular (non-evangelical) setting.

Other ADR Professional Practice

The field of conflict resolution actually trains a number of different professionals. Negotiators, Arbitrators, Facilitators, Victims Advocates, Police Negotiators and Mediators all fall within the practical training programs of dispute resolution.

These professions each have separate credentialing boards that govern and guide their respective practices. If you are not familiar with these professions, you have only to research on line to discover the many available private entities that train, credential and *provide* alternative dispute resolution service.

Negotiation & Facilitation

Negotiation is conducted by an individual who is advocating for one specific party in a dispute. The negotiator does not advocate for both sides simultaneously as a mediator does. The negotiator is paid by one side, but often attempts to find a resolution that will perceived as fair to both.

Facilitation is conducted by an individual with a group or organization that has problems pervasive to *many* inside the entity in question. The facilitator would work with a smaller group within that entity (i.e.: a committee from a school board) to resolve the issues brought and generate an action plan for implementation by that group or organization.

In general, professionals (who provide negotiation and facilitation) practice within the realm of "secular" dispute resolution. This is not to say that an evangelically trained professional cannot simultaneously obtain training and credentials as either a negotiator or facilitator, because this is often the case. However, when an evangelical professional assumes the role of either "negotiator" or "facilitator," he would do so in the capacity of a secular professional. In some dispute resolution professions, a more objective focus is called for.

The professions of negotiation and facilitation use a structure that assists both individuals and organizations to address problems. These practices employ a systematic approach to working through the issues presented. Trained practitioners must adapt to every changing aspect of the dispute, as an agreement or action plan is developed.

Arbitration

Arbitration involves the presentation of a dispute by two entities (usually a business and client) for resolution by a credentialed professional arbitrator. The practice of arbitration is generally focused in client/business disputes, and more often does not lend itself to new evangelical professionals.

Arbitrators must be credentialed and they act in many capacities as a judge. In arbitration, a dispute is brought to an arbitrator. The arbitrator hears both sides, and makes a decision as to what he feels will settle the dispute equitably. An arbitrator's decision may be *binding* (final) or *non-binding* (able to be brought later to a regular court of law).

Many companies (*for example: credit card companies or cell phone companies*) specify (in their contracts signed with clients) that all disputes between client and company will be settled by an arbitrator. Most arbitrators are attorneys but some non-attorney arbitrators are credentialed to offer services. It is important to note that many credentialing entities have long waiting lists for arbitration training and certification and fees for this professional training and testing can be high. The referral list for professional arbitrators can be difficult to join.

Mediation

The field of mediation is actually vast. The types of mediation available to the public range from a settlement oriented approach (on the legal end) to a more "transformative," approach (on the opposite end of the spectrum). See chapter seven for descriptions of mediation types and styles.

Table 9 - Types of Mediation Best Suited for Secular Intervention

The Types of Mediation Best Suited for Secular Practice include but are not limited to:

Insurance Claim Mediation
Class Action Settlement Mediation
Consumer Arbitration Disputes
Corporate Negotiations
Landlord Tennant Mediations
Building Contractor/Client Mediations
Mediated Settlement Conference
Contract Negotiations

Criteria for Secular Mediation

There may be other disputes that are better suited to secular practice that I have left out. In my research, I have attempted to locate the most prevalent types of mediation in existence today, but it is possible that there are areas in the United States that have mediation norms that I have not come across in my research.

As noted above, the most pervasive criteria for excluding a type of mediation to secular practice would be the requirement of the professional to have extensive knowledge of judicial statutes and practices.

In some cases, (as in family settlement mediation) a disputant may confer with his attorney and obtain the necessary legal information. Collaborative attorneys can offer many excellent options for resolution. However, many types of mediation do require extensive court intervention and knowledge of court protocol.

Pastoral Mediation, *Without* Attorneys Present

One option a pastoral mediator may select in such cases would be to conduct mediations with both sets of attorneys (for both sides respectively) present. William Ury (Fisher, Ury, & Patton, 1991) at Harvard's Law School's Program on Negotiation (PON) pioneered this type of mediation. Dr. Ury, himself an attorney, has successfully developed a method for conducting such types of mediation.

Mediating *with* attorney's present requires a more directive style and approach. This book has not provided a methodology for the provision of mediation with attorneys' present. Although, it is possible to utilize the skills outlined in this text with attorneys in the room. I want to reiterate that these methods were not designed with attorney mediation in mind.

In my experience, mediations that involve both attorneys throughout the process also involve the "agenda's" (motivations) of the attorneys respectively, unless the attorneys subscribe to collaborative efforts. The attorneys often take over the mediation by speaking for their clients, therefore, the direct statements and feelings of the clients are lost to attorney paraphrasing and sometimes attorney motivations.

This is not to denigrate this form of mediation. It does indeed have its place and benefits to clients. However, the pastoral mediation approach that this work presents does not "dove-tail" into the provision of mediation with attorneys' present. These types of mediations are best left to secular mediation practice because of the expectation of a deeper knowledge of court protocols and the unavoidable advantages that the attorneys may have over the pastoral mediator with regard to legal statutes.

Caution: Mediation as a *Tool* for Attorneys

Attorneys often use the mediation time to rehearse an impending court case and engage in negotiation. They are able to learn valuable pieces of information from the clients that they are able to use in court, and they may further run the danger of entrenching the disputants deeper in dispute.

This practice can obviously either help the disputants or hurt them. The problem lies in the fact that each opposing attorney possesses opposite goals, and when these two sides meet in mediation, their attorneys' separate sets of goals *clash* and the disputants can pay the price for this in many ways.

For instance, if the case is destined to return to court, one disputant could lose their advantage (through the loss of valuable information which is now no longer confidential) in court. No matter what happens, the court case will be altered by the attorneys if they are allowed to be present in the mediation.

The Benefits of Attorney Led "Negotiations" in Mediation

Some disputes actually do benefit from such interventions (building contract disputes) because disputants would have had such discussions anyway. Do not allow attorneys to manipulate *pastoral mediation time* with these negotiations. Pastoral mediators should stay out of attorney driven mediation and focus their time with disputants alone when possible.

The potential for pastoral mediators to help disputants to heal the other aspects of their disputes can outweigh these material exchanges. To stimulate emotional healing for the disputants is equally valuable to the resolution of their dispute. The emotional resolution is just as important in secular mediation. It exists on a level above the attorney negotiations (which focus on the material aspects of the suit).

Attorneys have a valuable place in the resolution of property disputes. Mediation can open another avenue for exploration of property settlement with attorney's present. Court based mediation can save disputants time in legal fees, if progress can be made toward resolution, and if this is the best practice that will suit the disputants' legal needs.

Power Imbalances – Not for Any Type of Mediation

Conflicts that would not be suited to mediation include marital conflicts that contain domestic violence. The power imbalance is biased toward the abuser (just by definition) and the potential to harm rather than help is double. The mediator must keep the power balanced in mediation – and there are ways to do this – *but* these simple methods do not work with the domestic abusers – whose impulses to manipulate are too strong.

In situations in which one party is automatically subject to another, mediation becomes either not an option or a difficult challenge. See chapter one for more information.

Positive Secular Focus

There is a time and place for everything, and in some disputes, a non-religious focus serves those in conflict best. Pastors may be the first professionals that a set of disputants seek to resolve conflict. However, after assessing the variables involved in the dispute, the pastor may determine that secular mediation would best address the problems presented. Do not force a dispute into pastoral mediation if it does not serve the needs of the disputants. Sometimes, disputes are best settled with secular intervention.

Most secular mediators practice their craft with caring motivation and benevolence for their fellow man. There will be times when we must simply trust this to be true, and allow those with legal and judicial knowledge to resolve the disputes that come the pastor mediator's way.

Part IV

The Gifts of Pastoral Mediation

Chapter 14

*And I have filled him with the spirit
of God, with skill, ability, and
knowledge...*

- Exodus 31:2

Approaching Mediation with A
Spirit of Resolution

Internal and External Experiences of Conflict

At its core, a conflict is an **internal** process experienced on multiple levels
that drives an *external* realization of a problem or larger conflict. The individual's *perception* and experience of the external conflict brings up the
deepest of his/her own pains, struggles, and shortcomings.
These internal perceptions stem from times when one was not loved *through*
growth and change in the way he/she needed to be. These pits of pain build
up within individuals silently, lying dormant until the stimulus of conflict
brings these feelings alive once again.

Internal Conflicts Drive the External Experience

Sometimes, it is a simple challenge that brings up these internal conflicts.
Individuals begin once again to experience unresolved pain left over from
his/her past and begins once again the journey to resolve his/her own internal obstacles.

At the same time, individuals experience the *external* conflict. The **external** experiences of conflict are where individuals "air" their internal challenges. As good as one could be at masking his/her true feelings in both business and personal settings, what individuals actually succeed at most is hiding his/her most raw and unfiltered emotions. Conflicts uncover these masks.

Conflict, in its truest experience, evokes the most "raw" of emotions.
Often one misjudges the perceptions he/she has when they see "raw" emotions being expressed. One judges these as conflicts that have the least possibility of being resolved, when actually the reverse is true. Individuals who are expressing the most "raw" of emotions are actually the closest to both the danger of violence and the possibility of resolution.

A Spirit of Resolution

A **spirit of resolution** is a "frame" a mediator can utilize from his/her first interactions with disputants to focus the discussion throughout the entire mediation process. Mediation seeks to promote a specific outcome; it seeks an agreement reached in a *positive* spirit of resolution. A spirit of reconciliation and caring can assist the resolution of any conflict. Some disputes simply need this "spirit of caring and reconciliation" to be not the primary focus of interactions.

Quiet but Caring Optimism

A quieter undertone of positive resolution is much more beneficial. A subtle but strong air of caring creates an atmosphere of respect and recognition. This allows disputants to focus their verbal energy on the more difficult aspects of their dispute. To use such a process, a mediator can embrace a *guided* approach in every occurrence of communication with both sides separately and together (refer to chapter eight).
To approach a conflict with a spirit of resolution is often the opposite of what disputants feel coming into mediation. Both sides have likely had moments of wishful thinking – wishing that they could find a way to resolve their conflict without further hurt to themselves and even to the other side.

Silent Hopes

Disputants come into mediators because they do not know how to resolve their dispute without fighting; they do not know how to bring up difficult issues in a manner that will affect resolution instead of provoke deeper conflict. However, disputants have silent hopes that they will be able to resolve this dispute well. Neither wishes to hurt the other. They both remember that they once cared much for the other; they just do not say so.

They both are aware of how much pain they have felt and on an unconscious level, they are aware that the other has had pain as well. It is hard for disputants to verbalize such feelings. It is important for the mediator to help disputants realize their silent hopes for positive resolution. It is best to not directly ask disputants if they have these feelings, nor suggest that they have these silent hopes, as this may immediately provoke disputants to deny such thoughts and feelings.

Stimulating Silent Hopes

A denial of this nature can cause disputants to "dig-in" or become more entrenched in their opposing positions. The best manner to stimulate silent hopes for positive resolution is to relay a story of how "two other disputants" had similar feelings. You may choose to relay the following story as an example during the right moment in the mediation.

TABLE 10 The Story of Jackie & Jonathan

The Story of Jackie and Jonathan

Jackie & Jonathan Jones were a couple (fictional) who divorced in 1998. They began the divorce process as many others did at that time, by getting attorneys and filing motions for dissolution of marriage. Their two children were 14 and 17. For 6 months, their attorneys exchanged paperwork, and Jackie & Jonathan exchanged frustrated e-mails, then Jackie read an ad on line about divorce mediation.

Jackie and Jonathan disagreed on how they were going to split up their furniture and home but they had agreed wholeheartedly that the best interests of their children were for them not to fight in front of them. In every mediation meeting, they sat, mostly silent. Their communications with each other were hostile and short.

There exchanges in mediation went something like this:

Mediator: "So what do you think you should do about the living room set?"

Jackie: **"You know I my mother bought that living room set. I want it."**
Jonathan: **"Your mother didn't make the last half of the final payments on it, I did.**
It's mine."

The mediator immediately recognized that both disputants had pent up anger toward each other and were venting this during the mediation, since they did not communicate outside the mediation setting. The mediator further realized his own mistake in asking for solutions. He recognized he was indeed assisting them to "dig in" to their respective positions, rather stimulating them toward a resolution.

Mediator next asked: **"Sounds like this is one thing you agree on,"** *the mediator smiles and writes the agreement on the flip chart. Both disputants smile, despite their frustration.* **"Let's table this discussion for now, and move to the discussion of the residency of the dogs."** *The mediator recognized that both sides had "dug in" to a stand still and that if they continued to pursue the discussion in that frame of mind, they would be right back where they were before coming into mediation. A change of perspective was needed, and writing their positions as an "agreement" was one method of shaking them out of their present mindset.*

As their discussion of residency of their two dogs began, the mediator noted that a change had occurred in the disputants. They talked in a more caring manner to each other, when the subject shifted to focusing on their shared pets that they both loved. *The disputants realized that they truly cared about their dogs and actually, had once cared about each other. They began to remember to consider the other person's perspective. By re-focusing them on something they both shared and truly cared about, they were able to remember how much they truly did agree to the perspective of the other side and silently hoped for another opportunity to state that. It was then the mediator's job to provide them that opportunity or recognize it when it came back up.* **Jonathan brought up the living room set in the next hour and offered to work out an agreement with Jackie to fairly divide this property. The offer was brought up in the middle of another discussion.** *It was the mediator's job to recognize this and remember it. The mediator made a note of it and* **respectfully began writing the offer on the flip chart. Later, the mediator wrote a point of agreement on his legal pad based on the ideas written on the flip chart. These points were refined and eventually became part of the mediated agreement.**

Negative Feelings

Disputants enter into the mediation process with anger and confusion. There are negative feelings of blame present from both sides toward the other. There are equal measures of both disappointment and the need for punishment of the other present on both sides.

To stimulate a positive spirit of resolution is an accomplishment in and of itself. The mediator must constantly focus himself in a positive mindset and *believe* that this positive focus is influencing the *disputants* to embrace a more positive mindset as well. **If you believe in the positive side of this resolution, then disputants are more likely to follow where you lead.**

Raising Difficult Issues

Throughout the mediation, *neither* side may acknowledge their pain, feelings of blame, punishment fantasies of the other, shared disappointment, or moments of positive focus but *both* sides have these feelings. They may hold it all in and show you something else. Conflict has this affect on people. In a state of crisis, *many* feelings show on individuals' faces. Sometimes, no emotions are visible, because people in conflict are in a state of transition. So wait and consider carefully before assuming anything from their facial responses.

Disputants go through many emotional changes during mediation. They need frequent breaks and snacks to give them time to process all of the things they are both feeling and doing. It is your job as the mediator to stimulate them to feel safe. When disputants feel safe, they will bring up their negative issues, trusting that you will create a positive environment in which they will be able to resolve these feelings.

It is the professional mediator's job to also raise difficult issues and know how to process them slowly. Approaching a dispute from the beginning with a spirit of resolution can positively influence the *entire* process.

Chapter 15

The tongue that brings healing is a tree of life...

- Proverbs 15:4

Pastoral Mediation:
Inspiration, Ministry & Healing

A pastor seeks to inspire, minister, and heal. *Inspiration* for the future, *ministering* in the present and stimulation for the *healing* of past wounds form the goals of evangelical leadership and for our purposes, for the pastoral mediator as well. These goals (inspiration, ministering, and healing) embody a future, present, and past reflection of any dispute. Disputes have roots in all three states of being.

Inspiring Positive Change

Pastors inspire. It is an unwritten job requirement. Members of a congregate become members because the pastor inspires them. There are other reasons individuals and families join a congregation, but if the pastor in question does not inspire them, they will not join.

If a pastor can inspire individuals to believe that they can positively emerge from a conflict, he has succeeded in the first step of his objective of inspiration. The pastoral mediator has the ability to focus all interactions from the first meetings, on a more holistic set of goals that have the potential for healing. People seek inspiration because they need someone to stimulate them to realize the best in themselves.

Inspiration means to motivate a person on a *non-verbal* level to begin and complete tasks and objectives that they thought were either unattainable or beyond their reach. Often, individuals know that they have the capacity to do something, but are not able to find something larger than themselves (and the seeming mundane nature of the task) to inspire them to take *on* the challenges that life presents.

Inspiration does not ignite fear. Those who use fear as a means of stimulation motivate others by force. Motivation by force is not healthy and never produces natural growth. If growth is the other side of conflict, then *inspiration* is the driving factor that stimulates *conflicts* to turn into positive experiences of *growth*.

The Soul of Ministry, A Guide to Mediation

To minister to a set of souls in need is a good and faithful gift. Many pastors providing ministry today also serve as pastoral counselors. Counselors often borrow from the field of ministry in their work, because many counselors believe that a deep relationship with a higher power helps guide them in their work.

Carl Jung, one of the founders of the contemporary practice of counseling had a famous wooden panel over the door to his office. Carved in wood, the nameplate over his door read, "Whether bidden or unbidden, HE is with us" HE meaning God. The feeling is clear, Jung felt that whether we asked or not, God was always with us and he wanted to convey (by placing this over his door) that God was always with him, as he gave his very human best to help those that came to see him for guidance in the worst moments of their lives.

To provide ministry in the *present* to individuals in conflict and crisis is work that must be ground in a deep and genuine love of the greater good for one's fellow man. Ministry like mediation is often spontaneous; it is immediate, and it is powerful. Ministry embodies caring and helps in the moment that the other person comes to you in weakness. Good mediation must also seek to provide such service. Ministry is selfless, and when it is selfless, it guides a pastor's practice of mediation.

I Will Lift Up Mine Eyes
Healing Old Wounds & Helping to Prevent New Ones

To provide stimulus for healing is divine. We never know from whence cometh our strength to be of assistance to others (Psalms 121:1). When we, any of us, are presented an opportunity to kindly give of ourselves in selfless effort to help heal another in need, this instinct seems to emerge from deep inside of us.

Personally, over the ten or more years I practiced counseling full time, I prayed without ceasing. Often while listening to others in need, I prayed that it be God that guided the one sentence I got in edgewise to ask – to stimulate healing. I know He did, and I always had the holistic healing of spirit, mind, body, and better social functioning as a goal –as do many counselors. For the past ten years, I have been a mediator and held on to these same guiding principles.

Although mediators help their disputants best when they constantly refocus them back to the tasks and goals at hand, mediators can and do stimulate healing to both disputants over the issues of conflict. As professionals, mediators help those who are not able to break down a problem into solvable parts – to do just that. By assisting disputants to see, *solvability* where they used to see impossibility empowers them to realize that larger, more holistic healing.

Mediation from Spiritual Inspiration

In essence, this book serves as both an overview of the field of mediation and a training manual for pastoral mediators but I hope it has gone much farther than this. I hope the establishment of this new specialty of pastoral mediation will inspire new and existing secular mediators to realize the skills they possess to affect better resolutions.

Adding the specialty of pastoral mediation combines one profession (ministry) that is focused in positively changing peoples' lives with another (mediation). Healing the emotions of those in conflict was one of the original intents of mediation, and I believe that a further development of these original goals continues.

Chapter 16

I will come and speak with you there, and I will take of the spirit that is on you and put the spirit on them. They will help you carry the burden of the people so that you will not have to carry it alone.

- **Numbers 11:17**

Of Spirit & Positively Focused Goals:
Summary of Pastoral Mediation Theory

In the latter part of the 20th century, a group of courageous professionals began an innovative journey. In a spirit of bravery and passion, they began a revolution within the American justice system.

Professionals (from the fields of law, sociology, psychology, and ministry) felt that the litigation practices in existence at that time in the United States were no longer serving the needs of the American people for justice and appropriate dispute resolution. They proposed alternative dispute resolution options that would better address the conflicts that so often wound up in the court system.

These individual professionals came together in communities. Judges, ministers, retired attorneys, and counselors all joined in this movement to reform the methods that were being used to handle disputes. Disputes were not actually being resolved, they were being processed through call and response in court. In the mid 1960's it was realized that *processing* a dispute and truly *resolving* it had become two different things. I believe that we have not veered far from that 1960's realization. The efforts of mediation theory and practice to date have firmly *established* the field of alternative dispute resolution. Now it is the job of contemporary mediators to continue to improve it.

An Original Spirit of Justice

Justice implies an equal resolve of conflict for *both* opposing sides. This is the ideal. The reality has become *justice* for the best-paid legal representation. The spirit of positive resolve that drove the creation of the field of mediation is the same spirit that we had all but lost in the mid twentieth century, as the field was slowly absorbed back into the statutes of law. The need for consistency and regulation is understandable and well founded. The address of conflicts, which are filled with vague emotions and unique problems continue to daunt the legal profession.

As this twenty-first century begins, the improvement of mediation practice to *better* address the hidden aspects of conflict beckons. Our ideas of justice have changed little; however, court protocols continue to encroach upon mediation practice. State statutes now heavily govern the delivery of mediation practice, and this noble profession runs the danger of returning to call and response court procedures.

Unfortunately, those who would most benefit from mediation, the disputants, have the least heard voice. Their emotional priorities during a time of conflict are elsewhere. If mediation is to answer the call for justice in the twenty-first century, it will take innovative mediators, dedicated to better practice to make this happen.

The Emotional & Spiritual Aspects of Conflict

Our emotions make us uniquely human. They encapsulate what is best and worst about us as a species, and our emotions manifest themselves most prominently in times of conflict. Emotions cannot be holistically addressed with mediation practice that is limited by *bottom-line* protocols for court resolution. To address the emotional issues embedded in conflict, one must understand the silent and invisible emotions that lie within.

The anger, sadness, disappointment, frustration and elation that is present in a dispute help disputants understand why their conflicts exist. We (as professionals) must seek to understand the emotional aspects of conflicts and validate the existence of these feelings – so we may help disputants to find holistic resolution. In this way, mediators will more thoroughly address the *material* aspects of each dispute when placing agreements in writing.

Understanding the Emotional Aspects: Better Mediation Practice

To understand the spirit of a conflict, one must go on a journey with the disputants – down the road of where they have been and experience each opposite perception of that conflict through the stories told by each disputant.

Each dispute will be different. Each will be a challenge that has no foreseeable solution, for if there had been an easy solution, the disputants would not have sought assistance. To provide disputants with a caring ear and kind understanding of the emotions in their dispute is truly a valuable service.

Healing & Growth, A Wonderful Extra Gift

Mediation is not focused in the *specific* stimulation of personal healing and growth. It is a wonderful extra gift that often occurs because of the mediation process, but it must not be the goals of mediation. For, if these were the goals of mediation, then the practice would simply be another version of psychological counseling.

Counseling is a wonderful field and sustains the society well on its own. I look forward to a day when the stigma associated with counseling is completely removed, because the profession truly helps those in our world who seek it earnestly. The separate goals embedded within the mediation process also serve the society well.

Positively Focused Goals

When the entire mediation process is structured to promote positive mutual goals, the disputants are free to express negative emotions without fear of retribution. The mediator's creation of a positive focal point for interactions creates a destination for their journey, assuring them that frustrations and failures are expected and the ability to set things right is within their reach.

Disputants are more likely to hold fast to their own ability to find a mutually beneficial solution in positively focused mediation. The mediation process outlined in this work describes a method for assisting disputants to set positive goals that benefit everyone. The work requires commitment on the part of the disputants toward an equitable resolution.

A Better Practice of Mediation

Since its inception, mediation has sought to stimulate a better resolution to the human disputes brought into the court setting. The field was founded in noble ideals. The path by which professionals have journeyed to provide the best service has been a noble one as well. The journey continues.

Mediation is a highly skilled profession that can truly change people's lives. Professionals need to be very confident in their skills and adept at providing them before attempting to provide mediation. The attainment of professional mediation skill through registry, certification, and other forms of credentialing is integral to the provision of mediation. Remember, the consequences of the work completed in mediation will be felt by the disputants (and their families) in the *years* that follow your experience with them. Assure that you have mastered these skills before you begin. You can do it. God will help.

Epilogue

To God belong wisdom and power;
counsel and understanding are His.

- Job 12:13

Past Uses of Terminology

The term "Pastoral Mediation," has held at least two opposite descriptors in recent years. Most publicly, the term was used to describe an unfortunate and painful set of resolutions – involving alleged pastoral sex abuse - for want of the best terminology to describe it. In many ways, the initial use of this term, "pastoral mediation," was a misnomer.

Establishing "Pastoral Mediation" Titling

The use of the term "Pastoral Mediation," was first established (according to the research of this author) by George Croft (1964) in an article he wrote with this terminology in his title. Later, Reverend Emerick-Cayton (1993) expanded the use of the terminology of "pastoral mediation," in his book, *Divorcing with Dignity*, (Emerick-Cayton, 1993).

Because of Tim Emerick-Cayton's (1993) courage to pioneer the use of his practice of mediation as "pastoral mediation," a bridge for a new specialty in mediation was forged. I based the establishment of this specialty of "pastoral" mediation on the work that had already begun toward this end by these two innovative professionals. Others may exist and may not have been located by this author.

The distinction between my use of the term "pastoral mediation" and its prior usage, which today is better described as "pastoral advocacy" is important. To begin a new specialty, conflicts in titling and terminology need to be discussed and accepted. It is my intention with this work to stimulate such a process.

Some Past Uses of the Term Pastoral Mediation

The meetings, organized between priests and victims of alleged sexual abuse in the Catholic Church, constituted a groundbreaking precedent of *acknowledgment* for the childhood victims of these crimes. The public acknowledgment of the *possibility* that a sex crime could have taken place in the church setting (for many involved in these sad experiences) *began* the process of healing. No established title for the meetings that were taking place between church leaders and victims existed.

Online news blogs ran stories in the year 2003 that used this titling (pastoral mediation) to refer to the on-going process of resolution that was being sought by priests and victims. The titling was popularized by the news stories of the time, but was not an accurate description of what was taking place. Today, this on-going resolution process is more accurately termed as "pastoral advocacy."

The Challenge of Terminology

Reporters and news story analysts often do not have access to more specific professional terminology for describing such events and often utilize the terminology that has been repeated by members of the lay public around the event.

In the heat of 24 hours news journalism, reporters write quickly to supply fast and interesting news coverage. It is not difficult to understand why reporters would utilize a repeated descriptor to characterize such an innovative set of practices by the Catholic Church. It was indeed a valiant step for the church to initiate this process and a challenge to describe it.

Pastoral Advocacy, a More Accurate Descriptor

The use of the term pastoral advocacy builds upon the established practice of "victim's advocacy," that has been practiced in professional police criminology for a number of years. This professional work arranges meetings between individuals alleged and confessed as perpetrators with victims of crimes including rape and murder.

The practice of spiritual resolution (between alleged victims and priests) continues upon the writing of this book in 2008, and is a valiant pursuit of emotional resolution for these victims and alleged perpetrators. In many documented cases, the perpetrators have been convicted of criminal sexual abuse and the process of having these perpetrators available to the victims of the crimes they were convicted of is actually an established professional job position in many community service organizations around the country.

The practice of victim advocacy within police departments nationwide has held critical success for many decades. This professional practice also employs professionals (usually specifically trained in local counseling centers) to "advocate" (stand up) for victims rights – through the court system. It is an admirable field that is highly acclaimed by those individuals receiving service from victims' advocates.

Victims' Advocacy

Advocacy, as it is used in state and national judicial and social systems, refers to professional individuals who support victims of alleged domestic abuse.

The term **victims' advocacy** refers to the professional practice of assisting *victims* of a crime to resolve their negative experiences with their alleged and convicted *offenders*. To assist individuals who have suffered severe consequences because of criminal activity has been a long-standing objective of most community counseling centers as well. Community counseling centers often employ professionals to assist victims of domestic abuse as victims' advocates.

Pastoral Advocacy with Former Pastors

A second use of the term "pastoral advocacy" has emerged in recent years to define a set of organizations that assist pastors who have left churches. These organizations help pastors to find another church to lead *or* help pastors to leave the ministry. This specific use of the term "pastoral advocacy" is in no-way connected with the practice of pastoral advocacy for victims of sexual abuse.

Their terminology appears to note their desire to support and assist pastors. This is another valid use of the term, "pastoral advocacy," and in the view of this author can be utilized simultaneously with "pastoral (victims) advocacy," as both terminologies serve opposite members of the public. It is unlikely that the public will be confused by these uses of the term "pastoral advocacy," because both will be clearly defined by the professionals choosing to use this terminology.

Pastoral Mediation: A New Specialty in the Field of Mediation

The field of mediation still works to establish clarity and acceptance within the popular culture. The need to make clear that this specialty of mediation does indeed fall within the established profession of mediation is important. New specialties of mediation are added each year. With this research, I submit the theories to establish the new specialty of Pastoral Mediation.

It is my hope that all of the 50 states of the U.S. and countries internationally will accept this specialty of mediation for use in local, national, and international communities. This theory of *pastoral mediation* may be used (with cultural adaptations) to provide mediation to individuals of faith worldwide.

Appendix A

Common Mediation Forms

Confidentiality Statement
Anytown Mediation

15 E. Church Street, Suite E
Anytown, State 12345

A "mediator" shall mean a person (not related to the dispute) who enters into a written agreement with the parties to assist them in resolving their dispute.

1. All work prepared by the mediator shall be confidential and not subject to disclosure in any judicial or administrative proceeding involving any of the parties to any mediation.
2. All mediators' case files (to contain all information of the aforementioned mediated case) shall be confidential and not subject to disclosure in any judicial or administrative proceeding to which such materials apply.
3. Any communication made in the course of and relating to the subject matter of any mediation shall be confidential communication and not subject to disclosure in any judicial or administrative proceeding.
4. Any statements made in the presence of such mediator by any participant, other mediator, or other person shall be confidential communication and not subject to disclosure in any judicial or administrative proceeding pertaining to any case involving mediation participants.

Dated this ___ Day of _____, 20 _ _

_____
Participant

_____
Participant

_____
Mediator

_____
Mediator

_____
Witness

(This document may also be notarized if so desired or required by the state court system in which it may be referred. Notary signature & seal to the right of signatures)

Agreement To Mediate
Anytown Mediation

15 E. Church Street, Suite E
Anytown, State 12345

This is an Agreement between _____, _____, and _____ "mediator," to enter into mediation with the intent of resolving all issues regarding: _____. The parties and the mediator understand and agree to the following:

1. Appointment of Mediator

The parties hereby appoint and retain _____ as mediator for their mediation. The

parties understand that _____ is not an attorney.

2. Mediation is Voluntary

All parties here state their good faith intention to complete their mediation by an agreement. It is understood that any party may withdraw from or suspend the mediation process at any time, for any reason or without stated reason.

The parties also understand that the mediator may suspend or terminate the mediation, if the mediator feels that the mediation will lead to an unreasonable result, if the mediator feels that an impasse has been reached, or if the mediator determines that he can no long effectively perform his facilitative role.

3. Definition of Mediation

The parties understand that mediation is an agreement-reaching process in which the mediator assists parties to reach agreement in a collaborative, consensual and informed manner. The parties understand that the mediator's objective is to facilitate the parties themselves to reach their best agreement. The parties also understand that the mediator has an obligation to work on behalf of all parties and that the mediator cannot render individual legal advice to any party and will not render therapy nor arbitrate within the mediation.

4. Legal Counsel

It is understood that the mediator has no power to decide disputed issues for the parties. The parties understand that mediation is not a substitute for independent legal advice. The parties are encouraged to secure such advice throughout the mediation process and are strongly advised to obtain independent legal review of any formal mediated agreement before signing that agreement. The mediator may come to require one or both parties to have their agreement reviewed by legal counsel to ensure that each party is reaching a reasonably informed agreement.

5. Mediator Neutrality

The parties understand that the mediator must remain impartial throughout and after the mediation process. Thus, the mediator will not champion the interests of any party over another in the mediation nor in any court or other proceeding. The mediator is to be impartial as to party and neutral as to the results of the mediation. The mediator will seek to reveal any operative biases that may come up and will disclose all prior contacts with the parties and their legal counsel.

Agreement To Mediate
Continued

6. Confidentiality

It is understood between the parties and the mediator that the mediation will be strictly confidential. Mediation discussions, any draft resolutions and any unsigned mediated agreements shall not be admissible in any court, administrative or other contested proceeding. Only a mediated agreement signed by any parties may be so admissible by the parties' free choice. The parties further agree that no subpoena shall be issued to the mediator to testify concerning the mediation or to provide any materials from the mediation in any court or other contested proceedings between the parties. The mediation is considered by the parties and the mediator as settlement negotiations. All parties also understand and agree that the mediator may have private caucus meetings and discussions with any individual party to promote resolution. In such case (caucus), all such meetings and discussions shall be confidential between the mediator and the caucusing party(ies), unless the parties agree otherwise.

7. Mediation Fees & Payment

The parties and the mediator agree that the fee for the mediator shall be $250 per hour for time spent with the parties and for time required to study documents, research issues, correspond through telephone calls, prepare draft and final agreements and do such other things as may be reasonably necessary to facilitate the parties to reach full agreement. The mediator shall also be reimbursed for all expenses incurred as a part of the mediation process.

A payment of $_____ toward the mediator's fees and expenses shall be paid to the mediator along with the signing of this agreement. Any unearned amount of this retainer fee will be refunded to the parties. The parties shall be jointly liable for the mediator's fees and expenses, unless otherwise documented by the parties themselves below.

As between the parties only, responsibility for mediation fees and expenses shall be:

_____ . &/ Or _____

The parties will be provided with a monthly accounting of fees and expenses by the mediator. Payment of such fees and expenses is due to the mediator no later than 15 days following the date of such billing, unless otherwise agreed in writing.

With my signature, I attest that I have read, understand and agree to the terms set forth in this document for mediation of my dispute.

DATED this __ day of ___, 20__

_____   _____
Participant   Notary Public

_____
Participant

_____
Participant

_____   _____
Mediator   Seal

_____   _____
Witness   My Commission Expires On (Date)

Memorandum of Understanding

15 E. Church Street, Suite E
Anytown, State 12345

Mediation Agreement Between

(name of disputant party(ies) **A**_____

(name of disputant party(ies) **B**_____

   DATE Written: _____

The above parties agree to the following:

_____
_____
_____
_____
_____
_____
_____
_____
_____
_____
_____
_____
_____
_____
_____
_____
_____
_____
_____
_____
_____
_____
_____

(Contents here may be typed, handwritten, or saved in document or printed. This document may be inclusive of several pages. The **Footer***: "Page___of___" is placed on all pages. Place a* **Header** *of: "The above parties agree to the following:" on all pages.)*

Page 1 of ____

Memorandum of Understanding

EXAMPLE of LAST PAGE:

The above parties agree to the following:

_____
_____
_____
_____
_____
_____
_____
_____
_____
_____
_____
_____
_____
_____
_____
_____

*The following signature block would be placed at the bottom of the **last page**. Omit the waiver line at the bottom if client has an attorney.*

Parties: Date Signed:

_____   _____
_____   _____

Mediator(s):   Date Signed:

_____   _____
_____   _____

(The following waiver may be included or omitted.)

The initialing party(ies) waive the right to have an attorney review this agreement before signing it and understand that once all parties sign this document they are bound to its terms.

Waiving party(ies):_____

Page 1 of ___

Appendix B

State Credentialing References

State References

This list represents the best information available as of spring, 2014. I am providing a reference to each state's official court entity that governs the practice of mediation. *In a few states, an association for mediation is the only reference.*

In many states, an association for mediation exists *in addition* to that state's court system reference. Since these are often private entities, I did not include separate links to associations unless another reference was not available.

Alabama :

> **Alabama Center For Dispute Resolution**
> **Supreme Court Commission on Dispute Resolution**
> http://www.alabamaadr.org/index.php?option=com_content&task=view&id=26&Itemid=40

Alaska:

> **Alaska Bar Association: Alternative Dispute Resolution**
> https://www.alaskabar.org/servlet/content/1404.html

Arizona:

> **Arizona Attorney General's Office**
> https://www.azag.gov/search/node/mediation

Arkansas:

> **Arkansas Administrative Office of the Courts**
>
> http://www.arkansas.gov/government/agency-detail/administrative-office-of-the-courts

California:

Superior Court of California: CADR
 http://www.sbcadre.org/neutrals/ethicsmed.htm
See Specifications by Region

Colorado:

The Mediation Association of Colorado
http://www.coloradomediation.org/

Delaware:

Delaware State Courts: Superior Court Dispute Resolution
 http://courts.delaware.gov/Superior/ADR/adr_mediator_all.st

District of Columbia:

District o Columbia Courts
http://www.dccourts.gov/internet/globalcontentlocator.jsf

Florida:

Florida Courts
http://www.flcourts.org/search.stml?search=Mediation

Georgia:

Georgia Commission on Dispute Resolution
http://www.godr.org

Hawaii:

Hawaii State Judiciary
 http://www.courts.state.hi.us/search.html?cx=015176889377364375
695%3Aawlaikv1y0a&cof=FORID%3A9&ie=UTF-8&q=mediation&x=-
336&y=-251

Idaho:

Idaho Mediation Association
http://www.idahomediation.roundtablelive.org

Illinois:

Mediation Council of Illinois
http://www.mediationcouncilofillinois.org

Indiana:

Indiana Association of Mediators
http://www.mediation-indiana.org

Iowa:

Iowa Association of Mediators
http://www.iamediators.org

Kansas:

Kansas Judicial Branch: Alternative Dispute Resolution
http://www.kscourts.org/Programs/Alternative-Dispute-Resolution/

Kentucky:

Kentucky Court of Justice
http://courts.ky.gov/courtprograms/mediation/Pages/default.aspx

Louisiana:

The Louisiana Academy of Mediators & Arbitrators
http://www.louisianamediators.org/links

Massachusetts:

Massachusetts Dispute Resolution Services
http://www.mdrs.com

Maine:

State of Maine Judicial Branch: ADR
http://www.courts.state.me.us/maine_courts/adr/index.shtml

Maryland:

Maryland Courts: Mediation & Conflict Resolution Office
http://www.courts.state.md.us/macro/becomingmediator.html

Michigan:

Michigan Courts: Office of Dispute Resolution
http://courts.mi.gov/administration/scao/officesprograms/odr/pages/
mediation.aspx

Minnesota:

Minnesota Bureau of Mediation Services
http://mn.gov/bms/mediation.html

Mississippi:

Mississippi Bar Association
http://msbar.org/for-members/mediators-directory.aspx

Missouri:

The Missouri Bar Association
http://www.courts.mo.gov/hosted/probono/Mediation.htm

Montana:

Montana Mediation Association
http://www.mtmediation.org

North Carolina:

North Carolina Courts: Dispute Resolution Commission
http://www.nccourts.org/Courts/CRS/Councils/DRC/Default.asp

North Dakota:

North Dakota Supreme Court
http://www.ndcourts.gov/Court/ADR/

Nebraska:

Nebraska Supreme Court Judicial Branch
http://supremecourt.ne.gov/5502/become-mediator-nebraska

Nevada:

Nevada Judiciary: Supreme Court of Nevada
http://www.nevadajudiciary.us

New Hampshire:

New Hampshire Judicial Branch: ADR
http://www.courts.state.nh.us/adrp/

New Jersey:

New Jersey State Courts: Mediation
http://www.judiciary.state.nj.us/civil/medipol.htm

New Mexico:

New Mexico Mediation Association
http://www.nmma.info

New York:

New York Courts: Alternative Dispute Resolution
http://www.nycourts.gov/ip/adr/divorcemediation.shtml

Ohio:

The Supreme Court of Ohio
http://www.sconet.state.oh.us/JCS/disputeResolution/FAQ/

Oklahoma:

The Oklahama State Courts Network: ADR
http://www.oscn.net/static/adr/default.aspx

Pennsylvania:

Pennsylvania Council of Mediators
http://www.pamediation.org

Rhode Island:

Rhode Island Mediator's Association
http://www.rimediators.org

South Carolina:

U.S. District Court of South Carolina: ADR
http://www.scd.uscourts.gov/mediation/guideline.asp

South Dakota:

South Dakota Unified Judicial System: Mediation
http://ujs.sd.gov/Programs_and_Services/mediators.aspx

Tennessee:

Tennessee State Courts: Mediation
http://www.tsc.state.tn.us/programs/mediation

Texas:

Texas Association of Mediators
http://www.txmediator.org

Utah:

Utah Courts: Alternative Dispute Resolution
http://www.utcourts.gov/mediation/

Vermont:

State of Vermont Judiciary
https://www.vermontjudiciary.org/gtc/Family/Mediation.aspx

Virginia:

Virginia's Judicial System: Supreme Court

http://www.courts.state.va.us/courtadmin/aoc/djs/programs/drs /mediation/home.html

Washington:

Washington State Dispute Resolution Centers
https://www.courts.wa.gov/court_dir/?fa=court_dir.dispute

Wisconsin:

Wisconsin Court System
https://www.wicourts.gov/services/attorney/mediation.htm

<u>West Virginia:</u>

West Virginia State Bar
http://www.wvbar.org/members/become-a-mediator/

<u>Wyoming:</u>

Wyoming Mediation Program
http://mediation.uwagec.org

Appended Bibliography

Assefa, H. & Wahrhaftig, P. (1990). *The MOVE crisis in Philadelphia: extremist groups and conflict resolution.* Pittsburgh: University of Pittsburgh Press

Association for Conflict Resolution. (2008, July 27). What is conflict resolution?

Retrieved   July   27,   2008,   from   http://www.acrnet.org/about/CR-FAQ.htm#whatisCR

Augsburger, D. (1986). *Pastoral counseling across cultures.* Louisville, KY: Westminster John Knox Press.

Augsburger, D. (1995). *Conflict mediation across cultures.* Louisville, KY: Westminster John Knox Press.

Bennett, S. (2002). *Arbitration: essential concepts.* New York: ALM Publishing.

Berecz, D. (2008). "This isn't your mother's divorce: you have options," Retrieved

December 10, 2008, from http://www.familyresolutions.us/options.html
Bible. (2008, December 1). Retrieved December 1, 2008, from http://bible.christianity.com/mybst/default.aspx?type=library&contentid=52759&category=REF

Bible Gateway. (2008, December 1). Retrieved December 1, 2008, from http://www.biblegateway.com/passage/?search=1Timothy%202:5&version=31

Biblical Quotes. (2008, September 9). Retrieved September 9, 2008, from http://biblequotes.wordpress.com/category/judging-others/

Boulding, K. (1990). *Three faces of power.* Newbury Park: SAGE Publications.

Bolton, R. (1979). *People skills: how to assert yourself, listen to others, and resolve conflicts.* New York: Simon & Schuster.

Brakel, S. J., (1974). *Judicare: public funds, private lawyers and poor people.* Chicago:

American Bar Foundation. Retrieved May 20, 2004, from http://web.lexis-nexis.com/universe .

Breslin, J., & Rubin, J. (eds.). (1999). *Negotiation theory and practice.*
Cambridge, Massachusetts: The Program on Negotiation at Harvard Law School.

Bush & Folger (2005). *The promise of mediation: the transformative model for conflict resolution.* New York: John Wiley & Sons.

Bush, R., & Folger, J. (1994). *The promise of mediation: responding to conflict through empowerment and recognition.* San Francisco, California: Jossey-Bass Publishers.

Cadence. (2008, September 8). Retrieved September 8, 2008, from http://www.thefreedictionary.com/cadence

Campus Library. (2008, November 20, 2008). Citing on-line sources using APA.

Retrieved November 20, 2008, from http://library.uwb.edu/guides/BusWeb/BusWebCiteOnlineAPA.htm

Clare, J., Roundtree, L., & Manley, E. (2003). *Alternative dispute resolution in North Carolina: a new civil procedure.* Raleigh, NC: North Carolina Bar Foundation and the North Carolina Dispute Resolution Commission.

Cloke, K. & Goldsmith, J. (2000). *Resolving personal and organizational conflict: stories of transformation and forgiveness.* San Francisco: Jossey-Bass Publishers.

Cortright, S. (2008). "10 Tips to Effective & Active Listening Skills," Retrieved September 8, 2008, from http://thelife.com/students/people/listen/?request_uri=/people/listen.html

Critical Cells. (2008, September 10). Retrieved September 10, 2008, from http://www.sciencedaily.com/releases/2008/08/080806184903.htm

Croft, G. (1964). *"Pastoral Mediation and the Psychology of Counseling,"* The

Heythrop Journal, Vol. 5, Issue 2, pp.178 – 187.

Denenberg, T.S. & Denenberg, R.V., (1981). *Dispute resolution: settling conflicts without legal action.* New York: Public Affairs Pamphlets. Retrieved July 2, 2004, from: http://web.lexis-nexis.com/universe.

Dictionary References. (2008, September 2). Retrieved September 2, 2008, from http://dictionary.reference.com/browse/closure

Divorce Source. [WDDC], (2008, May 26). Retrieved May 26, 2008, from http://www.divorcesource.com/TX/ARTICLES/schmitt5.html

Doyle, M. & Straus, D. (1976). *How to make meetings work: the new interaction method.* New York: Penguin Putnam

Duchan, J., & Black, M. (2001). "Progressing toward life goals: a person-centered approach to evaluating life therapy." Topics in Language Disorders, v22 n1 p37-49 Nov 2001.

Elmore, P. (2008). *Signs of closure.* Retrieved December 5, 2008, from http://www.paulelmore.com/blog/wordpress/?tag=signs-of-closure

Emerick-Cayton, T. (1993). *Divorcing with dignity: Mediation: The sensible alternative.* Louisville, KY: Westminster John Knox Press

Firestone, G., & Sharp, D. (2001). "Uniform mediation act," Retrieved 9-2-08 from:
http://www.law.upenn.edu/bll/archives/ulc/mediat/med0220.htm

Fisher, R., Ury, W., & Patton, B. (1991). *Getting to yes; negotiating agreement without giving in.* New York: Penguin Books.

Folberg, J., Milne, A., & Salem, P. (eds.).(2004). *Divorce and family mediations: models, techniques, and applications.* New York: Guilford Publications.

Frantz, R. (2008). "Chronic wound healing." Retrieved August 25, 2008, from
http://www.nursing.uiowa.edu/sites/chronicwound/Debride1.htm

Gerencser, A. (1995). Family mediation: screening for domestic abuse. *Florida State University Law Review, 23,* p. 43.

Grimm, J., & Grimm, W., Grimm, W.C., Grimm, J.L.C., & Zipes, J. (ed.). (2003). *The complete fairytales of the brothers Grimm.* New York: Bantam Books.

Gromala, J. (1996). "The use of mediation in estate planning," California Trusts & Estates Quarterly. *State Bar of California Estate Planning, Trust and Probate Law Section, Fall 1996.*

Hamilton, Margaret Wolfe (2008; 1878). *Molly bown.* London: Dodo Press.

Hart, T. (1980). *The art of Christian listening.* Mahwah, NJ: Paulist Press.

Hippocratic Oath. (2008, July 18). Retrieved July 18, 2008, from http://members.tripod.com/nktiuro/hippocra.htm

Hope, M.K. (2006). "Judging mediation: an assessment of the effectiveness of mediation programs in North Carolina," Published Dissertation on Disc. South Bend, IN: Graduate Theological Foundation.

Ivey, A., Gluckstern, N., & Bradford, M. (1982). Basic attending skills. Hanover, MA:
Microtraining Associates Incorporated.

June, L., & Black, S. (2002). *Counseling in African-American communities: Biblical perspectives on tough issues.* Grand Rapids, MI: Zondervan.

Justice, T., & Jamieson, D. (1999). *The facilitator's field book.* New York: AMACOM.

Kirchner, M. (2000). "Gestalt therapy theory: An Overview," Gestalt Global

Corporation. Vol.4 No. 3. Retrieved 9-2-08 from: http://www.g-gej.org/4-3/theoryoverview.html

Knights, W. (2002). *Pastoral counseling: a gestalt approach.* New York: Routledge.

Kolb, D., & Williams, J. (2000). *The shadow negotiation.* New York: Simon & Schuster.

Kreisberg, L. (2006; 2002; 1998). *Constructive conflicts: from escalation to resolution.* Lanham, Maryland: Rowman & Littlefield Publishers.

Lake, F. (2005). *Clinical theology: a theological and psychiatric basis to clinical pastoral care.* Lexington, KY: Emeth Press.

Lawler, M., & Roberts, W. (1996). *Christian Marriage & Family: Contemporary Theological & Pastoral Perspectives.* Michael Glazier Books.

Learn the Bible. (2004). "God is the judge," Antioch Baptist Church. Retrieved November 26, 2008, from
http://www.learnthebible.org/dp10208_ps75_1-10.htm

Lederach, J.P. (2005). *The moral imagination: the art and soul of building peace.* New York: Oxford University Press.

Lederach, J.P. (1997). *Building peace: sustainable reconciliation in divided societies.* Washington, D.C.: United States Institute of Peace Press.

Leehan, J. (1989). *Pastoral care for survivors of family abuse.* Louisville, KY: Westminster John Knox Press.

Little, A. (2007). *Making money talk: how to mediate insured claims and other monetary disputes.* Chicago: American Bar Association

Listening Skills. (2008, September 4). Retrieved September 4, 2008, from
http://www.taft.cc.ca.us/lrc/class/assignments/actlisten.html

LOC. (2008, July 10). Library of Congress Prints & Photographs. Retrieved July 10, 2008, from http://www.loc.gov/rr/print/catalog.html

Luchins, A., & Luchins, E. (1999). "Comments on the concept of closure," Retrieved 9-2-08 from: http://gestalttheory.net/archive/closure.html

McWilliams, J. (2008). "How is the mediator selected" Retrieved 7-3-08 from:
http://www.mcwilliamsmediation.com/articles_adroptions.htm

McGraw, P. (2000). *Relationship rescue: a seven step strategy for reconnecting with your partner.* New York: Hyperion.

Mediation Advantages. (2008, September 3). Retrieved September 3, 2008,from:
http://www.kinseylaw.com/clientserv2/famlawservices/familylawmediation/divorcemediation.html

Mediation Christianity. (2008, August 15). Retrieved August 15, 2008, from
http://www.divorcesource.com/TX/ARTICLES/schmitt5.html

Mediation in the United States. (2008, August 2). Retrieved August 2, 2008, from http://www.hg.org/arbitration-mediation-associations-usa.html

Miller-McLemore, B. (1993). "The human web: reflections on the state of pastoral theology," Chicago: The Christian Century Foundation, *Christian Century*: April 7, 1993.

Mitchell, V. (1998). Mediation in Kentucky: where do we go from here? *Kentucky Law Journal, 87.* p. 463.

Moore, C. (2003). *The mediation process: practical strategies for resolving conflict.* San Francisco: Jossey-Bass Publishers.

Moore, C. (1996). *The mediation process.* San Francisco: Jossey-Bass Publishers.

Motivational Quotes. (2008, August 30). Retrieved August 30, 2008, from http://quotes-motivational.com/Motivational/Divorce-Quotes.html

National Board for Certified Counselors. (2008, November 21). Retrieved November 21, 2008, from http://www.nbcc.org/stateexamination

National Victims Advocacy. (2008, July 14). Retrieved July 14, 2008, from http://www.trynova.org/

No Harm. (2008, July 18). Retrieved July 18, 2008, from http://www.geocities.com/everwild7/noharm.html

Nolan-Haley, J. (2002). Lawyers, non-lawyers and mediation: rethinking the professional monopoly from a problem-solving perspective. *Harvard Negotiation Law Review 7.,* p. 235.

Nolan-Haley, J. (1992). *Alternative dispute resolution.* St. Paul, MN: West Publishing Co.

North Carolina Mediation. (2008, July 7). Retrieved July 27, 2008, from http://www.nccourts.org/Courts/CRS/Councils/DRC/Default.asp

Passive Active Listening. (2008, September 4). Retrieved September 4, 2008, from http://www.learncustomerserviceonline.com/Preview/ActiveListeningCS/FrameMaster1.htm

Pastoral Advocacy. (2008, July 3). Retrieved July 3, 2008, from http://www.igfa.com.au/images/pdfs/Pastoral_Advocacy.pdf

Pastoral Advocacy Center. (2008, July 14). Retrieved July 14, 2008, from http://www.gardenministries.com/pastoral_advocacy_center.htm

Pastoral Advocacy Network. (2008, July 14). Retrieved July 14, 2008, from http://www.pastoraladvocacynetwork.com/

Pastoral Mediation. (2008, July 3). Retrieved July 3, 2008, from http://www.poynter.org/dg.lts/id.46/aid.18251/column.htm

Perls, F. (1973). *The gestalt approach and eyewitness to therapy.* Palo Alto, CA: Science & Behavior Books, Incorporated.

Plowden, Jr., E. (1993). "The judge's role in resolving disputes." *Georgia State Bar Journal, v29n4.,* p. 243. Macon, GA: State Bar of Georgia.

Resnik, J. (1992). *From "cases" to "litigation."* Santa Monica: RAND.

Rogers, C. (1959). "A theory of therapy, personality and interpersonal relationships, as developed in the client-centered framework." In S. Koch (ed.). *Psychology: A study of science. (pp. 184-256).* N.Y.: McGraw Hill.

Rosenblatt, R. (2006). "Essay explores the origin of the 'bottom-line,'" New York: MacNeil/Lehrer Productions. PBS Online NewHour, July 10, 2006. Retrieved December 10, 2008, from http://www.pbs.org/newshour/bb/entertainment/july-dec06/rosenblatt_07-10.html

Rothman, J. (1997). *Resolving identity based conflicts: in nations, organizations, and communities.* San Francisco: Jossey-Bass Publications.

Sandole, D., Byrne, S., Senehi, J., & Sandole-Staroste, I. (2008). *Handbook of conflict analysis and resolution.* New York: Routledge

Schnase, R. (2007). *Five practices of fruitful congregations.* Nashville: Abington Press.

Schwarz, R. (2002). *The skilled facilitator new and revised: a comprehensiveresource for consultants, facilitators, managers, trainers, and coaches.* San Franciso: Jossey-Bass Publishers.

Schwarz, R. (1994). *The skilled facilitator: practical wisedom for developing effective groups.* San Francisco: Jossey-Bass Publishers.

Shotwell, V., & Shotwell, R., (2008). *Thinking outside the box: life lessons learned from miracles with meanings.* New York: Wordclay.

Siegal, M., (2008). "First, do no harm." New York Post, June 22, 2008. Retrieved 7-18-08 from: http://www.nypost.com/seven/06222008/postopinion/postopbooks/first_do_no_harm_116584.htm

Snyder, J. (2005). *These sheep bite.* Babylon, NY: Appleseed Press.

South Carolina Mediation. (2008, September 10). Retrieved September 10, 2008, from http://www.scd.uscourts.gov/Mediation/guideline.asp

South Dakota Mediation. (2008, September 10). Retrieved September 10, 2008, from http://legis.state.sd.us/statutes/DisplayStatute.aspx?Statute=25-4-58.1&Type=Statute

Spangler, B. (2003). "Problem-solving mediation," Retrieved 8-9-08 from: http://peacestudies.conflictresearch.org/essay/problem-solving_mediation/?nid=1292

Spungen, D. (1997). *Homicide: The hidden victims: a resource for professionals,*
Vol. 2. New York: SAGE Publications.

Stringer, T. (2004). "Storytelling in mediation: the hero's journey," Retrieved 8-9-08 from: http://www.mediate.com/articles/stringerT.cfm

Susek, R. (1999). *Firestorm: preventing and overcoming church conflicts.* Grand Rapids, MI: Baker Books.

Sweedler, M. (2001). *Mediation theory and practice: lecture material*. Fort Lauderdale, FL: NOVA Southeastern University.

Tannen, D. (1986). *That's not what I meant: how conversational style makes or breaks relationships*. New York: Ballentine Books.

Ury, W., Brett, J., & Goldberg, S. (1993). *Getting disputes resolved: designing systems to cut the costs of conflict*. Cambridge, Massachusetts: The Program on Negotiation at Harvard Law School

Umbriet, M. (1995). *Mediating interpersonal conflicts: a pathway to peace*. West Concord, MN: CPI Publishing.

Uniform Mediation Act. (2008, September 8,). Retrieved September 2, 2008, from http://www.acrnet.org/uma/arewethereyet.htm

Van Yperen, J. (2002). *Making peace: a guide to overcoming church conflict*. Chicago: Moody Publishers.

Washington Mediation. (2008, September 11). Retrieved September 11, 2008, from http://www.washingtonmediation.org/howtocertify.html

Weeks, D. (1992). *The eight essential steps to conflict resolution: preserving relationships at work, at home, and in the community*. New York: Penguin Putnam.

Wilmot, W., & Hocker, J. (2001). *Interpersonal conflict*. New York: McGraw Hill Publishers.

Winslade, J. & Monk G. (2001). *Narrative mediation*. San Francisco: Jossey-Bass Publishers.

Wright, H. N. (2003). *Helping those who hurt: how to be there for your friends in need*. Minneapolis: Bethany House.

Zumeta, Z. (2000). "Styles of mediation: facilitative, evaluative, and transformative mediation." Retrieved 8-9-08 from: http://www.mediate.com/articles/zumeta.cfm